My Secret Life

My Secret Life

A Memoir of bulimia

Leanne Waters

Published in 2011 by MAVERICK HOUSE PUBLISHERS, Office 19, Dunboyne Business Park, Dunboyne, Co. Meath, Ireland.

info@maverickhouse.com
http://www.maverickhouse.com

ISBN: 978-1-905379-93-4

5 4 3 2 1

The paper used in this book comes from wood pulp of managed forests. For every tree felled, at least one tree is planted, thereby renewing natural resources.

A CIP catalogue record for this book is available from the British Library.

About the author

Leanne experienced severe bullying as a child, was very reclusive and quiet, often finding solace in writing. She suffered with mental illness from a young age, experiencing episodes of anxiety and mild depression. In her teens she suffered from bulimia nervosa and underwent several months of behavioral therapy. Her book, *My Secret Life: A Memoir of Bulimia* details that battle.

Leanne is now 21 years old and since that period, she has dedicated her time to her personal development, as well as her studies and writing. She is currently studying English at University College Dublin and works for the UCD *University Observer*. She hopes to enter into the field of journalism after completing her degree and go on to write both fiction and non-fiction titles. She lives in Bray, Co. Wicklow with her parents and siblings.

DEDICATION

To Mum and Dad, who remain the underlying bedrock of everything I am or ever will be. I love you both.

To my friends Anna, Kate, Ami, Emily and Roisin; without you, I never would have survived it.

To Nicholas, who kept me sane while writing this memoir. We got there in the end.

ACKNOWLEDGEMENTS

FIRSTLY, I WOULD LIKE to thank Michelle, a wonderful psychologist and an even better woman. Without you, I never could have made it through such a terrible time in my young life.

I would also like to thank my Granddad John, who instilled in me a most devout passion for writing. You have been an inspiration to me since I was a child and I will never forget all your encouragement and all your teachings about our shared craft of writing.

Furthermore, I was blessed to have been taught by three very special teachers throughout my education. Thank you to Mr. Enright, Ms. Dunne, and Ms. Traynor-Byrne. All of you saw potential in me when I don't think I truly saw it in myself. Whatever flair for writing I had before, it was because of you that I was brought to a standard of actually being able to publish this book. Thank you for believing in me. Finally, I would like to thank John Mooney, who took a chance on me and on my little story.

Contents

FOUNDATIONS

I HAVE NEVER LIKED the term bulimia. As human beings, we seem to feel the need to categorize everything and everyone. In doing so, we innocently attempt to better understand that which has undergone our necessary classifications. I, unfortunately, understand this more than most. But I dislike the term nonetheless. You see, once labelled, said thing or person must from that point onwards operate under that register almost exclusively. Like everyone else, I never wanted to be pigeonholed in any particular way, let alone by something like bulimia nervosa. Since accepting the reality of my condition, however, I find myself greatly altered and living what now feels like an accidental existence. I do not think, feel or behave as others do anymore. Instead, I think, feel and behave as a bulimic would. The distinction is all too evident both to myself and to others. Once the term itself has been applied, you are forever condemned to it. It shapes you, changes you and worst of all, it victimizes you. And for this, I hate it with a feverous passion. The problem is, in being bulimic I cannot fully be me; but without bulimia, there is no me.

And so, I have been seduced into not only accepting the term, but embracing it wholeheartedly to the very core of my being. I am bulimic. And everything about me is defined under that term; that often invisible umbrella which looms over all I do and everything I am.

Someone I used to love very much once told me that bulimia was merely an idea and that its existence was dependent wholly on the strength of mind of the given individual. It's not impossible that my pride is what prevents me from believing this argument. As if being bulimic isn't ego-wounding enough, am I now to accept that it's my own fault and simply a result of my own weak mind? I rather contend that it is my experience and now educated feelings that cause me to disagree on the matter.

But I suppose I do bear some of the responsibility, despite others having tried so tirelessly to convince me otherwise. It's natural for most loved ones to entertain the idea that none of this was my fault, particularly when blame and guilt have been such viciously active factors of the illness itself. But alleviating myself of all the responsibility is something I can't do. Because to a large extent, I secretly wanted this. Don't get me wrong, you don't exactly wake up one morning and say, 'I think I'm going to be bulimic from now on.' But once in the grip of it, you learn to embrace it like a friend, like your closest comrade and you would do anything to keep it safe. But we're getting ahead of ourselves now.

Naturally, I just can't bring myself to agree that bulimia is merely a notion or idea. An idea is something you conceive yourself. I didn't conceive this, or at least not consciously. Nor did I create it. Sometimes it feels like I was born with it, as if it were an organ in my biological make-up, inactive until recent years when it decided to make itself known. Yes, she had always been there; waiting, growing, learning. I have had no singular trauma in my life to cause her debut. People seem to think that that's exclusively why an eating disorder comes about, but not mine. I once received an upper-cut to the face for not giving a girl a cigarette that landed me in St. Colmcille's Hospital, but that's about it. If anything, I even relish in the fact that I can now say very truthfully that I can take a mean punch.

But I won't insult my bulimia by claiming that this or any other isolated incident gave birth to her being. You'll have to excuse my use of the term 'her'. I'm not simply addressing my bulimia as a man would a car, but am referencing it as I have come to know it. She is the person that lies deep within me; alive, almost fully formed and with feelings and beliefs as any other person would possess. And without her, I dare not think what would be left of me. This is part of the reason I find difficulty warming to the expression 'bulimia nervosa'. It's too clinical and does not give full credit to the weighty person she has become. She is more than bulimia. She is my other half and the darkness inside me that gives way to all my light. And for this, I will endeavour to never insult her. Even still, I sometimes wish I could protect her.

In order to find her foundations, we must go back to my own. Though it's difficult now to think of a time when she didn't exist, I am convinced that at some point in my life I must have been a person without bulimia. Or else, I must have been a person under some other, more appeasing, title. Perfectionist, high-achiever, anal-retentive; take your pick. I was once ranked among all of the above. I no longer consider myself any of these things but that question remains open to debate. I suppose, to a certain extent, I never did consider myself any of these things. If I did, perhaps I wouldn't have been so hell-bent in my pursuit of perfection in the first place. Indeed, it was this very pursuit that often justified my unhealthy habits and even the disease itself. Let me explain.

I am a person who thoroughly enjoys profiling. Though I don't claim to have any academic or psychological understanding to do so, more often than not, I will take an individual and mentally weigh up all I know of them to come to a conclusive decision on their character. The conclusion is subject to the current time and is variable; it can change with my growing understandings of the person, different experiences and of course, shifts in the traits of the individuals themselves. Now, I know what you're thinking; living with this girl must be hell. And you'd be right. It is rather excruciating living with me. Unfortunately, however, I can't get away from me. That established, you can now appreciate the agonising scrutiny I put myself under. But don't give me too much of your sympathy because as I've said, this is something I enjoy doing; or at the very least, it's something I've always done and have now just persuaded myself into believing is enjoyable. Upon personal reflection, I am no longer just one unit. I break myself into boxes and when separated, the contents of each may be better analysed and more closely examined. We'll take it one box at a time.

I am a very spiritual person. My faith is unyielding and ingrained so deeply into my very being that it has evolved into an invisible limb that works with and similarly to all others. Spirituality, therefore, is a very notable box. To perfect it and all it stands for, I am a practising Catholic. Despite its apparent unpopularity among my own generation, I attend weekly mass, say bedtime prayers and every now and again will even bother to read a particular scripture that my mother has come across and suggested. Furthermore, I'm proud of this. Though I make no attempts to boast about something so private, I relish in this ideal. I am Catholic by chance of upbringing but by contrast, my faith is something entirely internal and honest, untouchable even. As such, I am proud of the perfection with which I have tried to facilitate that faith. This box, consequently, is full. And if such an occasion arises that calls this perfection into question, the entire box will be upended, re-evaluated and altered if necessary.

The same rules would apply to my 'intellectual' box, if you will. Being successful professionally, academically and even intellectually was something I had valued very highly from a young age. It is true to say, that how we measure the above is dependent on each of us as individuals. I measured such things through high grades in school, extensive reading and striving towards what I believed would be a financially rewarding job. And I was often triumphant. Your typical pompous know-it-all, I was the perfect student my entire life. I worked, over-worked and took independent study as seriously as anything taught in the classroom. I read everything I could and especially titles that were known for their notoriety if nothing else. I told myself that I was bound for renowned glory in my chosen field of work and that it would, surely, pay me substantially. My parents, who had never enjoyed the luxury of furthering their own education and whose pockets were as empty as our fridge at home, nurtured my ambitions. While they struggled, I dreamed. Pumped with determination, I never again wanted to feel the heavy guilt of knowing that for the little they had, my parents gave me everything in their power. As long as they could provide me with the means, I would work until I could change our lives. And I did; even if for the worst. For almost the entirety of my academic life, this box was stellar.

You're starting to get a picture now, of how I operate mentally. Apologies for what will appear like a sense of self-importance; I assure you, it is mere neuroticism and nothing more. But what we are currently discussing forms the bedrock of the mentality that brought me so effortlessly and comfortably to the state of dysfunction that was to dominate such an imperative time in my life.

To further prove this, I will address just one more box, one more facet of grave significance. This is my appearance. It is here we find one of the many justifications I invented both to fuel and conceal my bulimia and everything she wished of me. It was this box that contributed to bringing about the extremist methods undertaken in my obstinate pursuit of perfection. If I could control and champion all other aspects of my life, this would be of no exception. So you see, though my aesthetical make-up was always relevant, it remained a mere factor of a much bigger equation. Therefore, to say one develops an eating disorder because they are unhappy with how they look or what they weigh, is utterly invalid and insufficient. Indeed, while in the heavy fog of my bulimia, a friend said to me, 'But Leanne, you're a really attractive girl. You know you are.' Perhaps this was intended to dissuade me from what she believed was a chosen lifestyle. It would have never worked because this was not the problem in the first place and my friend could never have understood this. She had never experienced a friendship like that of mine with my bulimia. All that said, my appearance does play a huge role in all of this and the issue of my weight became the target that bulimia would unleash all her furious wrath upon.

It was an easy target, in hindsight. It had been something I had always struggled with and was one of my personal failures on my path to perfection. If anything could damage my flawless mental profile, it would be my weight. Like almost every teenage girl, I contended with a negative body-image. I knew all girls of my age harboured negative thoughts on their own appearances, usually invalid, but I was certain that their temporary worries could not match mine.

Mine bore authenticity and a reason for concern. I had somewhat of a misunderstood-complex whereby no one could have possibly understood the pain of having to live in my own skin. They didn't have the memories I had and surely could not have been carrying the load that I strung over my shoulders daily. It's amazing what people can convince themselves of. To put it all quite simply, I can recall my dear friend Anna asking me a difficult question. We were mid-argument about the issue of my weight when she finally yelled, 'How can you possibly think you're fat? Are you gone in the head?' Disregarding the latter of her statement, to which I'd say yes, sometimes I wonder if I am truly 'gone in the head', I thought only of one incident from a very long time ago.

I AM SIX YEARS old. Patrick is the cutest boy in our year; all the girls like to play kiss-chasing with him. He was very bold to a teacher not so long ago and left school. But he's back now and I can see him in the yard. He is talking to Sarah. She is my best friend in the whole world and made me a friendship bracelet last week. When she tied the bracelet around my wrist, she told me to tell her my biggest secret and that because we know each other's biggest secrets, we were best friends. I don't know what her secret is, maybe I forgot to ask her. I told her that I liked Patrick and wanted to play kiss-chasing with him in the yard. And now Sarah is talking to Patrick; she's asking him to play kiss-chasing with us. I'm nervous because I can't run very fast.

I'm standing at the yard gate by myself and looking at my new runners. Mum gave them to me on my birthday. She knows I still can't tie my shoe-laces so bought me ones with straps instead. Sarah and Patrick are laughing now, so maybe that means he wants to play. I am not allowed go over to them until they tell me to so I wait by the yard gate. The yard is the biggest I have ever seen. Everyone loves this yard. The boys are playing football and the girls are skipping. I tried to skip with them once but got caught on the rope and they don't let me play anymore. When the teacher found out, all the girls were in big trouble and were told that they had to let me play. I told them I didn't like skipping all that much anyway.

'Hello there, Leanne.' Ms Dunphy is standing over me now with her yard bell. She isn't as old as the other teachers and always smiles. 'Why are you over here by yourself?'

'I'm not by myself, miss', I tell her. 'I'm playing with Sarah.'

'Where is Sarah?' she asks.

I point across the yard at Sarah and Patrick. They look angry with me now and I don't want to talk to Ms Dunphy anymore. I wish she would go away.

'We're playing a game.' I tell her. But she isn't smiling as much now.

'What kind of game?'

'I can't tell you, Miss. It's a secret.' I smile as wide as I can but cannot look her in the face. I'm angry at myself for lying to Ms Dunphy but don't want Sarah or Patrick to get mad with me. Ms

Dunphy murmurs something to me about how she is my friend. I nod frantically and eventually she walks away. I'm glad she's gone but am scared now because Sarah and Patrick have been watching me. I wave to Sarah and the two start laughing again before finally Sarah waves at me to go over. I'm so glad that I don't have to stand by myself anymore and tug at my skirt because I know my cheeks are red.

'Tell Patrick what you told me,' Sarah orders with a gleeful smile. Patrick is laughing and I suddenly wish Ms Dunphy would ring the yard bell.

'Well, go on!' she says again.

'I don't want to,' I mumble. I have a lump in my throat.

'You're so mean,' Sarah exclaims. 'Patrick is our friend and you're excluding him. I'm telling Ms Dunphy on you if you don't.'

'I....I...I like you.' The words fumble their way out of my mouth and I keep looking at my new runners.

'I TOLD you!' Sarah screams and the two begin to laugh beyond all control. I don't know what to do so I pretend to laugh too. When I do this, Sarah and Patrick both stop sharply. They exchange looks and then glare at me.

'You're disgusting', Patrick says with a winced face. 'You're so fat.'

I shrug my shoulders and the pair continue laughing. Ms Dunphy rings the yard bell and Sarah takes my hand so we can go to line-up. When I'm standing behind her, she turns around and puts her finger to her lips. I'm not allowed tell.

I DON'T BEAR ANY ill-will to these people from my past. To do so would be petty and even more humiliating than that day in the yard. And so when Anna asked why I thought I was fat, I simply informed her, 'Because I am.' Opposed to the obvious truth of, 'Because I was told so and I'm not allowed tell you.' In this rather warped way, I saved myself just a little bit of dignity. Who wants to relive hurtful childhood memories, let alone actually place any degree of importance on them? Thank you, but on this matter I chose to opt for the road most travelled.

Trying to evaluate whether or not I was indeed overweight – or at least in need of shedding a few pounds – is complicated now. Time has a tendency to distort truth and as if my perceptions weren't distorted enough at the time, today I'm near bewildered entirely. I have made a point of consciously trying not to think too much on it. If I were to properly analyse the situation, I'd probably still say that I was overweight before beginning my bulimic descent. Even at my lowest weight whilst in the densest stage of my illness, I never saw myself as being that skinny. I still don't believe I was ever so thin as to have sparked concern. Since that time, however, friends have disagreed and maintained that I had reached a point of emaciation. Similarly, I learned post-therapy that my mother spent several nights crying herself to sleep as a result of worry for my deteriorating condition. Perhaps I'm just too close to the situation to judge accurately and it's all too natural for my opinion to be disenfranchised. At the same time, it often feels that I have been trained to believe I was emaciated.

It seems part of the expectations of recovery; firstly, to believe that weight-loss was unnecessary to begin with and secondly, to assume that after losing a substantial amount of weight you surely resembled a poster-figure for anorexia. Having been aware of these possibilities in the back of my mind, I underwent a degree of resistance to recovery. I thought that if bulimia had brainwashed me into thinking I was too big, recovery was going to try brainwash me into thinking I was too small. And I didn't want that. *We* didn't want that.

Like anyone else sharing a life with an eating disorder, I sought to encourage myself. I traipsed for hours through pictures of bone-riddled women for motivation. The pictures were the perfect *thinspiration*, or *thinspo* as they are so affectionately entitled. All the while, my bulimic self would whisper sweet nothings in my ear and tell me that this was the definition of perfection. In looking like this, surely my 'appearance box' would be immaculate. During the months spent in therapy I once joked to a friend about how if I'd had a choice, I wished I had been anorexic and not bulimic; at least then, I could have looked more the part. She didn't get it and the joke, as it turned out, didn't go down well. But it was a thought that stayed in my mind long thereafter.

There is a misconception that anorexia and bulimia are the same thing. They're not. To a certain extent, I've often wondered if one exists without the other, as both retain similar behaviours. But I would never refer to myself as anorexic, mostly because I have never looked anorexic. A poor reason to define one's illness but it's just how my head works or at least did for a very long time. The truth is, bulimics such as myself tend to be an average weight. I lost and regained in the region of about 50lbs within a matter of two to three months. This pattern continued over and over again for two years. But I never slipped too much below average weight or indeed above.

In this way, bulimia satisfied all it needed to internally but never showed so much as to land me in hospital or worse, in trouble with the people around me. Evidently, it all came out eventually. That goes without saying. Before that, however, it enabled me to live a dual life in absolute secrecy. Of all eating disorders, bulimia is one of the most invisible. She was my invisible self and together we lived a hidden life. She taught me to be a master of secrecy and I had never felt so empowered as when with her. It was the perfect illusion.

I cannot put a cap on this era in my life. It's impossible to say when an eating disorder begins unless rooted in a particular trauma which, as we have ascertained, was not the case with me. In terms of behaviours, my habitual tendencies had begun to change around the age of 17. I would have moments of weakness that led to episodes of vomiting but they were few and far between. It was vomiting, not purging. What made me note this distinction, I don't know. But I never saw it as anything more than a 'once-off' occurrence that coincidently occurred more than just once. It was not until I had turned 18 that I started really hearing her in my head and more importantly, that I started listening. Christmas was on the horizon and, refusing to straddle behind the game even before the gluttonous season itself began, I vowed to make use of the new gym pass that lay in a drawer beside my bed. Finding the motivation wasn't difficult when reminiscing on childhood emotions and events, as we have briefly touched upon.

I had not known what it was to look forward to sports days in school, or to wear a belly top and pretend to be the given pop star of the time. Rather, I was the very poster girl for obesity in children. Unable to run very fast or for very long, I dreaded physical activities in school with tremendous angst; often claiming to be sick or, in the case of an annual sports day, not even turn up. And so, despite the very concept of exercise resurrecting haunting memories of a fat girl lagging behind and forever being picked last, I charmed myself into entering a gym.

'Mum, have I put on weight?' I asked my mother one day.

'Oh Leanne, I don't know.' She sighed. It was the usual sigh that had been present since I first started wanting to lose weight as a child. Having been slender her entire life, my mother didn't understand my concerns. She tried to sympathise. But more often than not, she was exasperated by the very concept.

'It's okay to be honest, I don't care. Just tell me.' I contested.

'Alright, fine. Yes, you've put on a little weight. But sure, you just need to exercise more and eat properly. I'll never understand this weight obsession with girls today.'

It was all the incentive I needed. If Mum had noticed a weight gain, surely everyone else had too and were trying to spare my feelings. I would not be the victim of their pity. I would not allow myself be seen as a failure. This thought in mind, I was slightly less encumbered on my first day in the gym. Instead, I was consumed by an unparalleled feeling of determination. Moments into my first workout, however, I felt that I had been humiliated even before my inevitable scarlet cheeks had time to flourish. Instantly, I tried to make excuses for my failure. I had not worn the correct clothing, so it was impossible to exercise properly. I had not fully clipped my hair back and therefore my fringe was sticking to my forehead. Had I eaten a meal before I came to the gym? Of course I had; that's why I was getting cramps. And everyone knows you simply can't exercise if you have a cramp.

Yet for all my justifications, I could not drown out that small voice at the back of my mind. *Lies,* she whispered. *Lies.* Her voice was all too familiar and not easily ignored. Upon brief consideration, I realised she was right and crumbled internally; not only for my inability to perform physically, but also for my attempt to excuse such a failure. The transition from my former state to the latter was a quiet one and took only moments. Yet its consequences were felt deeply and most severely. I left the gym and my zealous ambitions behind me and walked home.

Humility is something I have a lot of. Today, I relate it to the humbleness that rests with every thought I contrive, every word I utter and every breath I take. It is laced in my skin and is something that keeps my feet grounded to the earth when required. It acts as a prerequisite to everything I do and even keeps me firmly in touch with that inner self that people so often lose under pressure or when tested. The humility I possess today is a result of a practised exploration of thought, feeling and motivation. It was once, however, related to sheer mortification and nothing more. I have been humiliated more times than my pride would care to admit. The consequences of this make moments of embarrassment such as that detailed above all the more significant and all the more deeply felt. The shame that attaches itself to humiliation has never been easy to bear for me.

I AM VERY YOUNG. Every year for Halloween, my sister and I dress up as witches. My mum is very good at making a witch's costume. But this year we don't want to be witches, witches are boring now. My sister, Natalie, is dressed up as an Arabian princess. Her hair is long and silky and she's wearing make-up. I'm not allowed wear make-up because I'm too little. As the Arabian princess looks for her trick-or-treat bag, I put on my own costume. I am a dice. You know that thing you roll in board games? That's me. I'm in a cardboard box painted white with black spots on it. My mum has cut out holes for my head and arms. My legs are awkwardly manoeuvring somewhere down below, but I can't see them.

All limbs through the correct cut-outs, I proudly turn around to say goodbye to my mum. The blood rushes to my face. Natalie is looking at me through watery eyes and wearing a dangerous smile. She and her friends begin to laugh uncontrollably and I want to cry. I am humiliated. I clumsily rotate to Mum, whose eyes have fallen on my puce-red face with irrevocable pity and what looks like guilt. I want to yell at her for convincing me to be a dice. I want to tear away her painted box and stamp on it. I do neither of these things. To drown out the now hysterical laughter I would have to shout. If I do that, my voice will crack and I'll flush into tears. Instead, I wince at my mother and move out the front door in a sideways shuffle.

Natalie is supposed to trick-or-treat with me but she's walking with her older friends. I don't mind; I'm glad to be away from them. I have found several other children from the housing estate. I don't know them but they let me walk near the circle so it appears I'm not by myself.

I see the silhouette of our neighbour on his bike in the yellow streetlight. He's one year older than me but thinks he's too old to trick-or-treat. I don't like him. He cycles by me as I try to keep up with the other children. It's difficult in my box because the cardboard is rubbing off my underarms and my bag is heavy with sweets, popcorn, and chocolate. The other children don't want me to walk with them anyway, so they walk very fast.

He cycles by me and chants, 'Leanne the pan, the big fat man!' He's been singing that for as long as I can remember. He glides past me again, this time making me spill some of my goodies from my bag.

I hear laughing and see that the older boys – older than Natalie – are watching from across the street. I don't want to trick-or-treat anymore. I abandon my sweets scattered on the ground and carry myself and my bag up the street to my house. The big boys are still watching and I can feel their gaze sizzling on the back of my head.

I can hear the chain on his bike getting closer. He's cycling very fast. He knows I can't cycle without my stabilisers and he likes to show off. He's getting very close now. I try to walk faster but the box is starting to rub against my neck and my underarms are stinging. He starts chanting again and I begin to cry.

He cycles by again, this time even closer and says 'Whoooosh!' The next time he circles around I start to run. I don't care about my trick-or-treat bag anymore. I want to go home, away from the big boys and away from the boy on his bike with no stabilisers. I can hear his chain roaring up behind me now and I start to plead with the cold air in front of me to please stop him. Just as I let out a desperate moan from the lump in my throat, I hear the big boys laughing and before I know it, his bike pedal catches the back of my heel.

I scream and fall to the ground. My head doesn't slide out of my mother's cutting at the top of the box, but instead gets stuck halfway and I can taste cardboard and paint in my mouth. The palms of my hands are bleeding and I feel gravel bits falling off when I try to move them. I can't get up because the box is too big.

Suddenly I start crying hysterically and am ashamed of myself. I am ashamed because I screamed when I fell and now I'm crying. I know the big boys can see me and though at a distance, I can still hear the bike chain buzzing somewhere behind. I want to crawl into my mother's box and never come out again. I don't care that my underarms are stinging anymore or that my trick-or-treat bag is on the ground. I am no longer a dice. I am a girl in a big box and all I want to do is disappear in it.

I have no option but to crawl out of the box. I pull my arms in first and then my head. I try to wipe the tears away from my eyes but it makes my hands sting even more. The boy is gone. 'Look, look! There's a girl in that block of cheese!' shouts one of the big boys as I step out. I pick up my mother's box and my near empty bag and walk home. I won't tell Mum. I won't tell her about him, my hands, or the big boys. And, above all else, I won't tell her that they thought her dice was a block of cheese.

THE CONCEPT OF HUMILIATION, for me, has always been an illustrious element of my bulimia. Perhaps this is what has caused my now altered interpretation of it. The main reason for this is because it is something that my bulimia fed off throughout her persuasions. She used it to strip me down until there was nothing left. She would often dig deep to find either a moment or feeling of degradation in my past and succeed in applying it to my present. From there, an exchange of guilt and shame would take place. Until I would inevitably give in to her.

It didn't take her long to convince me to return to the gym. We both wanted it and knew above all else that we needed it. Suddenly, I was faced by what appeared to be a battleground. The question of dedicating myself to exercise was not – or at least no longer – about losing weight. It was rooted in the simple fact that I could and would do it. Not only would I do it, but I would be the best. I would be the fastest, the strongest, the person who could endure more than anyone else with whom I crossed paths. This was ambitious given the lack of exercise I had undertaken in recent years. But I found myself stuck on the word 'endure'. I could endure anything and I would endure everything to get what I wanted.

My return to the gym was not so horrific as I had envisaged. I worked through whatever humiliation I had created in my head and endeavoured to make use of what I saw as a terrible excuse for a human body. Being a smoker didn't help. I found myself gasping for breath after a few minutes. The trouble wasn't continuing on whilst panting and wheezing; it was hiding the evident exhaustion of my lungs from everyone else. It didn't matter about how much pain I was in, that was a mere inconvenience. What mattered was that no one knew it. I struggled but could hear that old voice in my head saying, 'Stop now and you know you won't start again.' It was never a voice of encouragement, not the kind that tells you you're doing really well. It was one of utter disgust. I was terrified to let her down. If I did, she'd never let me forget it.

I didn't care about this nonsense of 'warming up' and doing

stretches. Nor did I have any time for lifting weights or doing any form of resistance training. No, my concern was moving as fast as possible for as long as my body would allow. The more I moved, the harder I'd sweat and as each droplet rolled off, I imagined someone peeling away my skin, slice by thin slice. If enough could be peeled away, I would eventually be perfect. This was making me a better person. It was making *us* a better person. My breathing grew heavier and heavier and with every wheeze I suppressed, my lungs seemed to scrape against an invisible grater and tore away bit by bit. The girl jogging beside me seemed to do so effortlessly. She was a local girl whom I'd seen around town on more than one occasion. She was petite and slender and had a relaxed expression on her face, as if the gym was her home. She appeared to own both the room and more importantly, her own body. My body, on the other hand, was not my own. I would take one stride and it seemed the whole room thundered with the sound of my foot crashing down on the surface beneath it. It was as if I had no control over it or what it did.

How could I have let myself get to this point? Was I not the very definition of discipline? *Not looking like that*, I heard that voice whisper. I would just have to put up with it. Amidst the occasional whispers, the pounding noise of my feet and the squeaking of my inner thighs as they rubbed off each other, I jogged and eventually sprinted until my knees began to buckle. I would not stop until that girl had gone. In my head, we were in a competition and she would just have to quit first. Eventually she did. She relinquished her workout, effortlessly dabbed her forehead with a neat towel and glided out of the room as if nothing had transpired. *The audacity*, I thought to myself. And in that moment, for no apparent reason other than the contorted justifications that lay somewhere in the abyss of my mind, I wished that girl every bad fortune. The next time I would see her, surely she would be as grossly overweight as I and would never again quit a competition as she had just done.

We're not that weak. It echoed around my head again and again. Not long after this, I finally went home with my body aching and muscles beating. It was glorious. For every ounce of pain or discomfort, I felt liberated and there was a sense of validation like never before. I could do this and I could do it well. Naturally, gym attendance increased after this episode. In a very short period of time, I had become a regular. And unlike most regulars, my attendance had escalated from three or four times weekly to daily. Every morning, I cycled to the gym before the sun even had time to wake up. It would only take 15 minutes or so but it was the best part of my day. I felt more at ease in those early morning hours than at any other time throughout my day. It was comforting to be so alone and I experienced a strange sense of authority knowing that as the world slept – or my very little world at least – I was awake, alert and active. Often I would prolong the journey ever so slightly by stopping at the end of my road, just as you came into the town. There was a quiet brilliance about the town when it was empty. The ground still seemed warm from the people who had previously bustled their way around it and buzzed in muted excitement for the coming day. More importantly though, on those dark mornings the town was mine and mine alone. It felt as though it lay at my mercy and was a part of my internal kingdom. I controlled everything on those morning cycles.

My workouts would cease shortly before school began. They were relatively rigorous and generally finished with a swim. But it still felt insufficient. It wasn't long before I would begin returning to the gym after school in the evenings. In many ways, it didn't matter how much exercise I did, even if it was too much. Very rarely would a person say to you – or at least never was it said to me – that you are doing too much. More often than not, it went unnoticed in my case and on the rare occasion it was mentioned, I was congratulated on my hard work. And I cruised on this novelty for as long as possible.

Looking back, I consider this time as the calm before the storm. The evanescent life before then had been a time of planting seeds and while I trotted along, oblivious to the rapidly developing new mentality, roots had long since started to grow and stretch across the earth beneath me. The potential for such a disease to manifest had always been there and it was now coming to fruition, even if I didn't know it at the time.

It was around this point in my life that I started dating again. After a two-year relationship at far too young an age, I had enjoyed my single freedom as much as I could and lived my teenage life as one is expected; care-free and with little or no commitments. Though I reminisce on that first love with tremendous nostalgia and probably rose-tinted glasses, I was glad to be without a boyfriend at such a young age. But along with a changing mentality and growing insecurities, I had begun to crave constant reassurance. This emotional sanctuary was to be found in a local boy with whom before this point I had little or no connection. The son of someone I admired greatly, he appeared to have both the intellectual and emotional stimulation I coveted. The problem with young romances I have found is that they tend either to be incredibly nurturing or else terribly upsetting. There is no middle ground here and being as young as we are, people of my own age are near incapable of being able to judge a romance at the onset. Even still, I am only learning and doing so very slowly. This particular romance, as it would turn out, would be of the latter and would do more damage to my sensitive state than I could have ever imagined. It was impossible for me to know this at the time, however, and like all teenage girls I tactlessly launched my fragile feelings and all the weight they carried in at the deep end.

It must appear now that I take myself rather seriously. To a large extent I do. But the importance of this romance is not measured in how I felt for the other party; it is rather measured in the effect it would have on my mental condition and how it acted almost as the catalyst to my bulimic behaviours.

In the beginning, however, I was smitten. We were in many ways an unlikely match and as is natural for most after the passing of time, it's difficult to recall what caused the initial attraction. But it was there nonetheless. Friends and indeed family could not understand it but were nevertheless encouraging to anything that would promote my own happiness. It did this for a very brief period of time before turning sour.

I cannot blame this boy for what later happened; much of why the romance darkened was down to my own dependency. I needed the reassurance of him, an emotional home for my feelings to bed down in. I think I would have taken this in any way he gave it. Over time, as is natural, he decided to move on. My confidence deteriorated while his flourished. And yet as the dynamic shifted and solidified, my dependency only proved to grow needier and my insecurities consumed me. With each measure of my worth I gave to him, I took it away from myself. Eventually, I imagine, there was nothing left and I – the person I'd known before this – was gone. Something or someone had to fill the void, the emptiness. Thank God she was there, I once thought to myself. Thank God for her readiness, for her willingness.

I AM A TEENAGER. My boyfriend and I have been together for almost two years. I'm certain that I will never love anyone as much as I love him. I look at older couples a great deal and always note how they don't behave as we do. They don't laugh enough, or play or act in a silly way with one another. Apparently they take themselves far too seriously for that kind of nonsense. Or perhaps they just hide it all better. We feel no need to hide though. In fact, we hide nothing. I have never been this open before. I feel no need to keep any secrets anymore. I doubt if I'll ever have to keep another secret again.

Sometimes I wonder why on earth he wants to be with me. But the reassurance he provides is all too overwhelming and the thought is fleeting and never lasts very long. Now, more than ever, I think back on that day it all really kick-started. He knew how much I cared about him. Yet, being unsure of his own feelings, went abroad with family after telling me it was over. It had felt so final and I'd never been that upset before. Despite the temporary heartache, it didn't take long before I was seeing someone else. That someone was, in theory, everything a girl of my age should have wanted. I tried to put him to the back of my mind. It wasn't long however before he heard of these new developments. After receiving a rather frantic mail from him entitled 'Please', how could I not resume thinking of him? I'm not sure I'll ever forget the day he flew home; sitting together and talking about silly things that only we could talk about. He had come home for me and me alone. I had a clear choice and the question was all but answered before he'd even asked it.

People make this stuff out to be so complicated. Yet here I am still riding this perfect wave with the person I most want to be with. I'm not sure how anyone could think love is so difficult. This is love and it couldn't be easier.

I LOVED HIM AS much as any teenager could love someone. The love was youthful by definition and my perceptions on it have changed greatly over the years. Still, it was a happy time and marked one brief interval in my young life with a most glossy polish. This new romance, however, could not have been more different to what I had known before. Throughout the affair, I committed ardently to bettering and ultimately perfecting myself. If I could do just that, then perhaps I would not feel as I had come to since it had all started. Perhaps some of that confidence could be regained and that self-worth be dug up. But it didn't work.

I began exercising at night, long after the house had drifted off to sleep and I could be alone. It was in these hours that that familiar voice was at its loudest. I didn't just hear what she had to say, I felt it. I felt it in my skin, in my bones, in every strand of hair and eventually I would feel it so hard that my stomach would wrench itself up and hurt with each thought. Maybe I thought if I moved fast enough, I wouldn't hear or feel all those thoughts. Maybe if I made myself hurt in some other way, I wouldn't feel those pangs as my stomach curdled in disgust. So that's what I did, moved as quickly as possible until a muscle would ache, until my sides would feel like they were tearing and until I had caused just enough physical pain to mask any other. Oftentimes, the best thing to do would be to take some painkillers beforehand. It would mean I could prolong my exercise for a greater period of time. For every moment spent doing overtime, I enjoyed just a little extra allotment away from the reality of the nothingness

I had become. It was one of the best forms of escape in those quiet hours and required only me, and whoever now dwelled inside me.

It almost goes without saying now that by this stage, my eating habits had changed profoundly. Most people seem to maintain the mentality of 'Well, I can just burn off whatever I eat through exercise.' I, however, contended in the back of my head that if I ate too much it would surely have wasted all that time spent exercising. I began to eat much less. Generally it went unnoticed because the change wasn't initially all that severe. Eating became like a race against time. I would eat very small amounts and would time it around exercising. In this way, I could never give the food enough time to latch on to my insides. It was like I suddenly became aware of an invisible glue that lined my stomach. Anything I ate could stick to it almost immediately. The only way to stop this from happening would be to exercise before the glue had time to set or shortly thereafter. This process was fast which meant I had to be faster; I had to be one step ahead of my own body at all times. It was exhausting to say the least.

I watched any and every television programme I could that surrounded the issue of weight-loss. Mostly I just found that the programmes half spurned me, but half aggravated me at the same time. *Of course they can stay that skinny*, I told myself. *They have their own personal trainers and dieticians.* I started to develop a most curious relationship with the images I was seeing. The women portrayed on television and in advertisements represented everything I wanted to be; determined, disciplined and utterly perfect. I also, however, cursed their names and told myself that if these women were in my position, they surely could not look as they do. *They're not strong enough to go it alone*, I thought. But we were. If I could somehow get my head and my body in sync with one another, together we could do it with absolute perfection. Suddenly being flawless didn't seem so impossible.

It seems almost inconceivable now but I began searching the internet again and again with words and phrases such as 'skinny women', 'thinspo' (thin inspiration) and even 'emaciation'. I didn't want to be that skinny, though it would have been preferable to my size at the time. No, initially I just wanted to draw a contrast. I felt that I was one extreme and that by looking at women who lived at the other end of the spectrum, I could motivate myself enough to find a happy medium between the two. I was captivated by these images. Oftentimes, I would glare in horror at some of the extremities depicted but I could not look away; I could never stop myself looking that extra bit closer. Their bodies, unlike mine, could be studied like a painting. While my own felt like one massive surface of skin and filling, theirs were concave with protrusions scattered here and there. Their bones rose and fell from shadow to shadow, with porcelain skin draped over like silk. They were jagged creatures and were composed of sharp-edges and spindly bends, reminding me of a delicate spider. If you had a gentle enough touch, you could have played their ribcages like a piano. Tummies were always flat but evolved very abruptly into hips. With each image, a new twist and turn of the creatures could be found until I finally had a mental image of every possibly pose such a body could display. It was art. I would slip into a trance and would temporarily leave my own body looking at them. She who now lived in my head guided me gently from picture to picture and like a sponge, I soaked it all in with ease and what felt like nourishment. It was as easy as breathing.

The weight loss thus far had been minimal when taking into consideration how hard I had been working. Looking back now, I doubt any amount of weight loss would have proved sufficient at that time. I was nevertheless completely dissatisfied. I never again wanted to feel that way, never again wanted to feel so utterly inadequate. It was thanks to this sense of total incompetence, however, that a new fire was ignited within me. I now had an unquenchable thirst, which completely absorbed me from head to toe. What exactly it was, I couldn't put my finger on. But its presence created a ravenous appetite, not of my body but of my mind. It could not be satiated by any earthly sustenance. I was not interested in the origins of this hunger, my only concern was how to nourish it.

I am ten years old. I play Gaelic football on my school team. I don't really like it but everyone plays because you're weird if you don't. Besides, Mr O'Brien is our couch. He's also my teacher and the coolest adult I know. He doesn't talk to us like other adults do and everyone wants to make him proud. That's why we play. I'm not very good at football; the others can run faster than me and always seem to know what they're doing when we're on the field. I always stand near the goalpost and try to avoid getting in the way. I once tried to kick the ball but scored an own-goal for my team. Everyone was really angry at me that day and my other teammates didn't want to talk to me afterwards. I think they've forgiven me now but I don't want to make such a mistake again.

But this match is important. We've travelled all the way to the countryside by bus. Everyone has been singing and chanting all day. Some of the players' mothers have come along to support us. They've made sandwiches for half-time and painted posters to cheer us on with. I feel like I don't belong here. Everyone really wants to win and I just know I'm going to ruin everything. For the entire journey, I thought I was going to jump out of one of the windows. I also get travel sickness and now that we're finally in the changing rooms, I don't feel well. As everyone straps up boots and puts on freshly-washed jerseys, I cower under the pressure of what's to come. This is always the worst part. The room is buzzing with chatter and the hype of the atmosphere around me seeps inward, manifesting itself into panic. Every vessel and artery is pumping. I can smell the grass outside and the detergent used to wash all the uniforms. I hate these smells purely because they remind me of moments such as this.

'Are we ready lads?' shouts Mr O'Brien. There's a resounding cheer and a clacking stampede, as the studs scrape across the changing room floor. I try to essentially throw myself into the flurry of people in the hope of being swept along and forgetting my worries. I can't quite get in though and as usual, I slowly lag behind the bustle of players. I take one last look at the changing room and pray that I get a nose bleed to delay my appearance on the pitch. It doesn't happen and I trot quickly to catch up with the others. I wonder would they notice if I just didn't go out onto the pitch? Too late. We're given a quick pep talk before being marched out to our playing positions. I assume my usual spot near the goalpost and hover uncertainly near a member of the other team that I'm supposed to be marking. They have their back turned to me with their eyes no doubt fixed on the ball, waiting for everyone to get going. I awkwardly shuffle a little closer to make my presence known. The player, No. 11, briefly glances at me as if I'm a random spectator who has wandered onto the playing field. It clearly registers with him that I am actually his opposition and he moves a foot or two away. I'm not bothered staying too close to him because I don't care about this silly game anyway.

At long last, my agonising wait is over and I hear that dreaded whistle blow. The ball is thrown into the air and the roaring and screaming commences. I have never been comfortable with crowds. It's very overwhelming to hear that many voices joined in unison or, in this case, individually shouting things I can't comprehend and joining together to form one echoing noise of absolute chaos. *No wonder people think the Irish are mad,* I think to myself. *We sound like escaped mental patients*. I'm suddenly very angry with the mothers screaming their heads off and with Mr O'Brien spitting orders from the sidelines. If they care so much, why don't they just get on the field themselves and play?

'Leanne! What are you doing?' comes Mr O'Brien's voice. The ball has come to my end of the field and No. 11 is darting after it. 'Look lively!' he shouts again. I tremor and run as fast as my sausage legs can carry me. I have my eyes on the back of No. 11 but can't keep up. He's about to score and I slow down in pace because I just know I won't make it in time. I hear my teammates screaming at the top of their lungs because I'm giving up. Then I hear a reverberating 'YES!' flush all over the field. Kevin has snatched the ball from No. 11 and is now tearing up the field with it. Our team is saved for the moment.

After what feels like hours, it's finally half-time. There were a number of occasions when I was required to do something. Each time, however, Kevin or Richie or some other able teammate would step in and rescue me from total disgrace. Mr O'Brien is talking us through our performances and noting a handful of players in particular. He looks at me as if about to say something but quickly brushes on when he sees the look on my face. Poor man. Not only am I ruining his match, but he pities me too much to even tell me so. As the others contemplate the first half, I ask to be excused and plod down to the changing rooms. I feel as if everyone is watching me as I walk by; the mothers, the spectators and all the other children. I'm sure that they either feel sorry for me or are just laughing at me.

When I get to the changing rooms, I feel as though I'm going to burst in some shape or form. My forehead feels ablaze and my temples are pumping with blood. There is a lump in my throat and it takes every muscle to stop me from crying. I pace up and down, filled with a sudden fury, a sudden fire. Eventually I march from the changing rooms back onto the field just in time for the second half to commence. I missed the pep talk. Mr O'Brien shouts words of encouragement to me as I storm across the pitch. I barely hear him. I barely hear anything now. I must have missed the sound of the whistle blowing because the ball is up in the air. With no time for thought, I feel that fire blazing inside me and suddenly I am darting for it. I cannot feel my body, only my mind. I am a racing ball of white heat and air. And then suddenly, there I am with the football in my hands, wet and mucky; feeling has shot back into my arms and legs like a light bulb being switched on. *Too late now*, I think. And with no hesitation I sprint faster than ever before, carried by sheer desperation and the sound of the roaring crowd. I boot the football with a swift kick and it's soaring before finally it lands in the back of the net.

A moment of silence takes place and seems to cling to the air above us. It weighs down on me like a damp cloth and I shake nervously when I hear cheers and screams of exaltation. I look to the sidelines and Mr O'Brien is beaming, with his hands up in the air and the kind of smile I'd only seen on very rare occasions. I fill up inside. My glory isn't over and for the rest of the match, I tear up and down that pitch like never before. I feel like a tornado, consuming everything in my path; every time my hands grasp that ball, I feel as if I am going to eat it before finally belting it on. Today, even if just for one day, I am so glad I'm playing on the field. Back in the changing rooms after a knock-out win, everyone is cheering and congratulating me. The assistant coach, Mr White, names me player of the match. As the roars continue, I look to Mr O'Brien who stands in a corner. He is smiling a very quiet smile. The fire that blazed in me is finally starting to fade. I feel the last of its magnificent embers glow inside me. When I look back to Mr O'Brien's quiet smile, I see them glowing on his face too.

WHAT MOTIVATES ANY INDIVIDUAL to act in a particular way is often incredibly ambiguous. That fire that took hold of me so many years ago is the same now as it had ever been. The hunger and thirst I felt at the onset of this dark period had been there long before. It still hurts me to know that the fierce zeal which once brought about the happiest memories in childhood would eventually turn my life into a living hell. All that was required by this stage was a trigger.

It finally came on one weekend afternoon. I remember it had been a disruptive week. My confidence had been totally shot of late and, internally, I was falling apart. I had school exams to study for and as I worked hard for my grades, everything else fell by the wayside. I hadn't been to mass in almost three weeks, had read nothing but class textbooks and had started gaining weight. By the time the weekend came, I was happy to indulge in whatever was left of a silly little romance. When he and I did meet, however, I found he was colder than usual. He carried himself and his conversation in a most detached manner. When I probed about what was wrong, he dismissed it and said that all was well. And so, we carried on as usual, as any teenage couple would. The elephant in the room was ignored and it seemed to suit both of us perfectly. In theory, it was an extremely relaxing day spent enjoying our free time and privacy together. Practically though, something didn't feel right. When the day was starting to draw to a close, we stepped outside for some air and he moved away from me, his back turned.

'Are you happy with this?' he asked.

'With what, you and I?' I replied. 'Yes. Are you not?'

The conversation proved to be a long one. It was carried out through a series of harsh comments and sarcastic quips on both our parts. When I addressed several of the many things that had happened during the course of the romance, he showed little understanding. Indeed, he showed almost no concern for how it had affected me. Of course I can't blame him. We were just teenagers and this was just part of growing up. Moreover, he was unaware of the consequences of the things that had happened. It was impossible to have predicted such a future and neither of us had any idea of the creature that had been growing inside me for so long. It was this creature that would take every emotion until it was amplified beyond all recognition. Whatever I felt on the surface level, she seemed to feel it tenfold and more. She would take the feeling, magnify it and dwell on it until it would finally resurface under a new manifestation and under a new meaning. When she was through with her interpretations, that new meaning would slice through me until I finally fragmented. I would fall to my knees and sure enough, I would fall at her feet.

Eventually, the inevitable break-up discussion was coming to an end and while I was collected and composed on the outside, she writhed, twisted and fought with me from the inside. I had failed yet again and it tore me up from the inside out.

As I was driven home that evening, a strange transition occurred and when I finally stepped out of the car, I was now someone else entirely. Something had changed profoundly, though I didn't know it at the time. The conversion was a hushed one; it was delicate and so soft that I had not noticed it. Nevertheless, a metamorphosis had most certainly occurred. It took only moments but in those darkening flashes of time, I no longer stood as a full person. I had evolved into something more complex, something darker. A double-register seemed to form in my mind. From that point on, everything I would see, hear, touch or believe would be registered twice; once by me and then once by her, that darkness inside me.

In hindsight, it had taken many years for my bulimia to develop and it was the consequence of both my personal disposition and a series of rather unfortunate occurrences. Its roots lay in the deepest earth and stretched so far into me that I had grown with it, alongside it, even in it. It did not form in this moment alone of course; let us not lose our grip on reality just yet. No, its foundations had been laid long before this. It would be after this moment, however, that I – that we – would go on to make some of the most devastating choices in my life to date.

The Fast

The process of making the choices I did was an easy one. They were given little thought for consequence and as such were decided upon rather quickly. As long as my goals could be met in a speedy fashion, nothing else mattered. It was a time that allowed little scope for self-reflection. My vision for such things had become greatly impaired; my grasp on exactly who or what I was could no longer be easily defined. Perhaps I just didn't want to probe that deeply. If I did, I ran the risk of finding nothing. That would have been unbearable.

It is here that I suppose we must ask a most inevitable question: is an eating disorder an uncontrollable disease or is it a chosen lifestyle? This question has been answered in many ways by close companions and by strangers whom I have witnessed debating it through, usually with little knowledge or empathy for the condition itself. I'm sure most would contend the former and so would I to a large extent. It's difficult for me to believe that I chose this for myself, particularly when it has caused such trauma both to my own well-being and the people around me. At the same time, however, there is always at least an element of choice in such things. Mostly, it feels that though my bulimia was indeed a selected path, it was not I who made the decision. It was made by a determined alter-ego who had by this stage almost consumed me completely. I was at her mercy and as briefly touched upon earlier, I wanted to be. Attempting to for ever control yourself and everything in your life is a very exhausting endeavour. In a sense, I chose to hand over the reins and let her make the necessary decisions that I simply couldn't bring myself to do. It felt like a wonderfully natural way of going about things and allowed me to alleviate myself from the responsibility of having to ponder over such matters. As a result, the entire transition from the person I'd known before to the person I had become remains a very blurry one and ultimately lost through the distortions of time.

I do, however, remember the day I started a new fad diet. It was only days after the aforementioned evening. More than anything else, I felt an unwavering sense of urgency as if something terrible was sure to occur if I did not begin this diet immediately. To use the term anxious would surely have been an understatement in this case. I was a ball of nerves. The criticality of the moment seemed to swell up inside me until I felt like I was going to choke under the immediacy of what needed to be done. It wasn't too difficult coaxing my parents into allowing me start it; they had seen me cry over my physical appearance more times than they should have in my life and thought this may finally put a halt to my unyielding insecurities. The diet was simple; I drank three prescribed milkshakes a day and nothing else for a period of two weeks. The challenge of it was less daunting than it should have been, given I had reached a point of sheer desperation. I would have done anything. But by my fourth day of not eating I began to feel the strain of it. It's around this time that your body slips into a process called 'ketosis'. I never could get my head around its scientific idiosyncrasies and won't bore you with them now. What it meant for me, on a very basic level, was that I became extremely lethargic. Though I continued taking the shakes as required, as well as drinking up to two litres of water a day, I just could not find the energy to do very much at that time. My body was heavy and sluggish. I seemed to feel the weight of it more than I ever had before. It was more than just a mere awareness of my own limbs and muscles. It was as if I was trapped within myself. My mind – which before now had seemed capable to venture outside this body and into any earthly or otherwise crevice – was now firmly confined within the boundaries of it. And I thought of nothing else for those two weeks.

'It will be worth it', she told me again and again. For the sake of mild discomfort in such a short period of time, I wouldn't fail so haphazardly. This was easy, I told myself. And I pitied all the people who, like me, were currently endeavouring to lose weight and going about it at a slow or modest approach. I knew that they were doing so because they did not have the discipline I did, nor the commitment. They couldn't really want it, not the way I did. Otherwise, they would do as I was and would be more successful.

But nobody is like us. Nobody can do what we can. They're just not that strong, she reminded me.

The two-week diet came and went at an extraordinary pace. In hindsight, it wasn't even all that difficult to do. Though I wasn't consuming any food or beverages, I had enjoyed what I came to see as the luxury of those milkshakes. It wasn't much but it was sustenance nonetheless. I wasn't aware of what I was capable of doing to my body then and felt a temporary sense of accomplishment. But looking back now, I was naive and in the greater scheme of things, had only just touched the tip of a most complex iceberg. Nevertheless, I was satisfied at the time. In those two weeks I lost in the region of about 13lbs and coasted on an evanescent high of exaltation. It was about more than simply being physically lighter. I felt psychologically lighter, as if someone had finally set a match to all the cumbersome wax in my head and it was melting away, drip by drip. The somewhat superficial benefits helped too. I now had the freedom to dress in a way I couldn't before, to carry myself differently and to a certain extent, even behave differently.

For that very brief period in time, I seemed to reign as any other Queen Bee. From the inner workings of my mind, a hive formed. It was a sacred place and so intricately enclosed, so meticulously encased that it was my mine and mine alone. No one knew it existed. This was how to best preserve this hive inside me, as I knew that even the gentlest whisper could threaten it and it would surely crumble. Inside this place, in the safety of its impenetrable walls, I came alive and drowned in its sacrosanct honey. I sat on a throne of my own making and she, who had always dwelled in the changing shadows of my life, played the power beneath it. She was happy to do so, as always. While I savoured my time atop this throne and revelled in superficial attention and compliments, she churned and laboured relentlessly. You see, more than anything else, she now saw and understood the greater possibilities. It had only been a mere two weeks. But with those two weeks came new ideas. It was clear to both us after those two weeks that I had potential we'd never dreamed of. Before I could conquer the world, I had to conquer myself. After a two-week fast, suddenly this was possible.

I AM 13 YEARS old. I know most teenagers are known to have very bad skin but mine is exceptionally horrific. I've had acne on my face since I was very young and it just seems to get worse and worse as I get older. When I was ten years old, a boy ran up to me in the yard and told me that there's a solution for people like me called Clearasil Complete and ran back to his friends laughing. But I'm not sure how long I had acne before then. That's the earliest memory I have about my skin and I don't like to think about it all that much anyway. Mum always says that this happens to everyone, but I don't ever remember this with my older brother or sister. My sister Natalie, in particular, has had perfect skin her entire life. I've never seen a blemish or mark anywhere on her face. I got the worst parts of the gene pool and both she and I know it.

I pleaded with Mum to do something to help me. We went to the doctor and I was given Minocin, a prescription drug to help clear my skin. I've been taking it for quite some time now. My skin is better, but still not perfect. Sometimes I look in the mirror, very closely at my face, and I wonder what it would be like if I could simply take a few layers of it away. I imagine taking a scalpel to one of my ears and carving a very definite line from one ear to the other, all along my jaw. From there, I would peel back the top layer of skin, then the second and then the third, until all my acne was gone and my face could heal under a new blanket of immaculate parchment. I would never do it though. I get weak at the sight of blood and would undoubtedly faint once the smell of it hit my nostrils. But the temptation is there. Quite often, I get angry at the sight of my own face. In all its hideousness, I think it looks like a mistake and in many ways, I wish I could punish it for looking so grotesquely unnatural. I wonder if other people have these thoughts; if they look at themselves as I do, see a monster looking back at them and pray that one day, they'll be strong enough to kill that monster forever.

Maybe it's just my mood. I've been feeling terrible of late, like I've been sucked into a vacuum of complete sadness and I can't pull myself out no matter how hard I try. I suppose, I've started to give up on trying anyway. My family have noticed it too and keep passing comments like, 'You seem very down lately.' If only they knew how bad it has really gotten. Mum is keeping a very close eye on me; she watches everything I do now and I feel like I'm just waiting for one big explosion to happen. I'm not surprised she's so concerned though. I have been having a lot of trouble with the girls in my class. Mum says they're bullies and was in the school last week talking to my teacher about it. They don't understand it's my own fault though. If I wasn't such a teacher's pet and a know-it-all, then the girls would like me. I try really hard to say things I know they want to hear but it doesn't help make me popular. If anything, it seems to make things worse. They recently found out that I told on them because Mum contacted the school. Last week, a girl hit me in the face and said, 'Now go tell your mummy that!' and Mum went back to the school about it. I heard her and my teacher talking about everything that's been happening. I overheard something about calling the Gardaí into it. I hope that doesn't happen because I just want to forget everything. But now Mum won't let me out of her sight.

She can see that something is wrong with me. I always knew that something wasn't right about me and now everyone else knows too. I am crying in my room and she bursts through the door. She asks me what's wrong but I don't tell her because I can't. I cry a lot now and I don't know why. When I look in the mirror, I always need to cry even more. She starts going on about the Minocin drug; I don't know what she's talking about. Eventually, she says it has a great deal of side effects that she didn't want to tell me about. She knew how upset I would be if I wasn't allowed take them and didn't want to scare me. She mentions something about damage to my liver and other serious sounding things. But what I hear over everything else is the word 'depression'. The drugs can make you depressed. I was depressed and this was part of the reason why. It was why I had been crying so often and why Mum had been observing me so closely. It can't be easy being my mother. I would hate to have a daughter like me and I know my sadness and inability to be like everyone else must break her heart. If I could just be normal, her life would surely be a great deal easier.

I cry even harder now, not even trying to hold anything back. Mum fusses and shouts and tells me that I'm not to take the tablets anymore. She tells me I'll feel better soon, once they're out of my system. But I don't think so, I feel like it's too late now. It's as if this 'depression' is in my bloodstream now and I don't need the tablets to keep it alive anymore. I've seen the monster and now I'm sure of its potential. Had I not seen the existence of that monster in me, I would have never known its many possibilities. But now that I've seen it, I know it will be with me for ever.

Everyone interprets the word 'possibility' in their own distinct way and thus we are all aware of its presence in both our own lives and the lives of others. But it is only when it is cast into the realm of reality that we truly start to believe in its might. The power of possibility champions only when it becomes an actuality in our daily living. As a child, I never knew I was capable of succumbing to such devouring sadness. But once experienced, I knew that such a feeling had the potential to be there always and that even without feeling its existence in every waking moment, it was always possible thereafter. Equally, my bulimia required only the realisation of this word to come to full strength. It was unlikely that I would conquer myself in the manner I so desperately wanted to, but it was now possible. This was all my bulimia needed.

It only took a matter of weeks for this idea to gain authority and I consciously endeavoured to resist food whenever possible. It wasn't that I didn't believe I could lose weight through the usual methods of exercise and a modest diet; I knew this to be true, if not by my own standards obviously then by those of others. But the momentum of these tried and tested exertions just wasn't enough. They couldn't fill that growing void of nothingness nor satisfy the imposing hunger I felt. Such ventures required endurance, moderation and above all, patience. I seemed to have none of these characteristics. I'm convinced now that I can endure quite a lot but without a visible goal to light my path. More often than not, my commitment will falter and of course, this was the case with most of my weight-loss attempts prior to this time.

Moderation is another facet under which my character falls short. Friends often joke about my somewhat extremist nature. The truth of this only became apparent as I got older. Though it may seem altogether passionate and the trait of a rather romantic individual, my undeniable lack of moderation has proven to be one of my biggest obstacles in life. Whether in relation to my career, my finances, my relationships or indeed my varying pursuits for perfection; my natural tendency to go from one extreme to the other has often left me troubled, weary and completely heartbroken. It has proven to be one of the most self-destructive characteristics I showcase as a person and made the transition into my illness worryingly easy and almost comfortable.

This trait is closely linked with my inability to be patient. Time cannot contend with the speed of the human mind and the rate at which it manifests its brightest and most powerful ideas. It moves too slowly for that. Furthermore, I come from a generation of great velocity, in which everything is carried out at an exceptionally accelerated level. The importance of now is regarded above any other period it seems. Like most of my generation, I have always made huge demands on that 'now' and actually go as far as being shocked when such demands cannot be met efficiently. If time wouldn't wait for me, then I resolved to never wait for it.

'Losing weight takes time,' people told me. I would take nothing from time I decided, not when it already gave so little away. Some time was required of course, but I would insist it was minimal.

Skipping breakfast was effortless, as I had never really eaten in the morning anyway. During a number of diets, I forced myself to eat something healthy before the day kicked off; usually a fruit salad or very complicated dish I read about somewhere. Even then, I hated eating breakfast. The irony is, I have always seen myself as a morning person and was never able to sleep much later than about 9.00 am. But for all my claims of being a sunny person when first out of bed, apparently my stomach could never quite keep up. Consequently, it was a tremendous relief to consciously decide against food in the mornings. More importantly, it went unnoticed. I was never expected to eat breakfast because I never had and saw that part of my day as somewhat of a free pass.

The rest of my day would prove rather difficult without the milkshakes, or so it seemed at the time. Looking at that time now, I had it easy. If ever I tried to skip a meal now, more than likely, it would be a most futile labour; all my family and closest friends know about my bulimia and would make it impossible for me to do so. But again, we're racing ahead of ourselves now and best keep to the matter at hand. At that point, they were in the dark about the illness and I was too. So I suppose, I had a substantial degree of freedom. A simple, 'I already ate', would usually suffice for a while.

My family has never really been one functioning unit. We tended to unite only in crisis, like when a loved one died and a funeral would follow or when my sister and I fought. But in general, we were simply a collection of five individuals who happened to be tied every now and

61

again by this notion of blood. We slept, worked and operated all at different times and would, in a sense, merely bump into one another along our daily journeys. My father was a labourer who toiled more than he rested and was almost always in the National Rehabilitation Hospital, where he worked. My mother, the binding gel of this collection of parties, appeared to live on another planet most of the time. From working part-time to managing finances, shopping and the overall upkeep of the household, she lived in a world I was happy to be ignorant to. My older brother and sister were both employed and living the usual lifestyles of twenty-somethings, in one way or another. With a new son on the way and his desperation to lay down solid roots, my brother Peter featured very little in this time of my life and lived an hour's drive away from the family home. In the context of my bulimia alone, what all this meant was that we never ate dinner together. The concept of all these people sitting down together united around a kitchen table to share food was, and still is, a foreign one.

All this noted, dinners were still rather tricky. The temptation to eat would peak in the moments my mother was dishing up a meal, which she would usually prepare for everyone and leave in the oven to be eaten when convenient. I was never spurned by hunger alone, as I knew I could overcome the feeling with relatively little effort. No, I was spurned mostly by guilt. I hated letting my mother down and subsequently would become disgusted with myself for letting her hard work go to waste. At the same time, however, I felt I didn't deserve the fruits of her dinner time efforts. My father would eat after a heavy day of lifting and being on his feet and thus, had earned his meal when he came home at night. Similarly, my sister and mother were slim-figured and as a result deserved the food in front of them. I, on the other hand, couldn't seem to contend with these justifications and so resolved to the idea that I just wasn't worthy enough for these meals as they were.

I'm sure you're thinking that this is surely the most distorted logic you've ever heard and yes, it is. But it was my logic nonetheless and so blindly real that I could do nothing but behave under its dictation. Trying to figure out an escape route from all these thoughts was near impossible. And the only thing left to do would be the most obvious; escape the house itself and eat out. Of course, I didn't do this. It was as simple as informing my unsuspecting family that I was going out with friends for something to eat and would be home later. Often I was given money for these outings, which I saved to buy cigarettes and to pay into nightclubs when the occasion arose. I would call to a friend's house, claiming I had just eaten dinner and would proceed with my evening as planned. In the beginning, it was flawless and worked under perfect timing and execution. Naturally, though, it didn't last. There are only so many times you can tell your mother that you're not eating at home and only so many times you can bother a friend at home during dinner time. Even without the knowledge of my strange eating habits, others were still mildly suspicious. Or if not suspicious, they were at least curious about the growing eccentricities in my behaviour.

One peculiarity to be seen was my increasing need to be alone. In one sense, constantly being around others was just too inconvenient for me. I had never noticed up until this point how almost everything we do while socialising with other people revolves around food. Whether it was coffee and lunch with girlfriends, drinking on a night out with a crowd or having a movie night with close companions – which would finish with the inevitable phone call to order pizza or Chinese food – it seemed impossible to avoid eating while keeping company. It also demanded better excuses. 'I already ate', 'I'm not very hungry' and 'I've gone off that stuff' didn't really cut it after a time. I was eventually forced to become a little more honest, if not altogether sneakier.

I told friends a half-truth and informed them I was trying a new, very strict diet, in which I ate three meals a day. Obviously, snacking while with friends was unacceptable and this very simple excuse bought me some leeway from their probing questions. It didn't, however, buy me much with time and I was required to spend as much time with them as I had always done. If not to stay out of the house for longer periods, then simply to solidify a perfect facade that all was well and normal.

If keeping distance from my friends was difficult, it was even harder to do so from my family. Though we were in general a family that enjoyed our space, we lived in a small bungalow and were usually on top of one another. There was only so long I could shut myself away in my bedroom without drawing attention or concern. I used to do that as a child when something was wrong. Throughout my years of bullying, in particular, shame would drag me into a crevice in my bedroom and firmly shut the door behind me. The trait was unmistakable even at the age of 18 and I knew it wouldn't take long for my mother to begin her interrogative inquiries. I had to be more careful about the way in which I carried myself and conducted my behaviour.

Somewhere in the back of my mind, upon the throne of my internal hive, she seemed to always be one step ahead of me. And rightly so, as she knew better than I and we were both aware of this. Had it just been me living in my own head at the time, I probably would have tactlessly retreated from everyone and everything in my life, as was the usual case in such circumstances of turmoil. But this time would be different because I wasn't alone. While I sat at the driver seat, she controlled the hands at the wheel and steered me right into the heart of all undesired company. Compared to my naivety, she was a craftswoman and played games with meticulous strategy. And while directing my course was the overall objective, making it as undetectable as possible was part of the game.

For a while, she did this very well and I found myself catering both to her demands and the social standards of everyone else. I started living two lives; the one in my head that fed off both my thoughts and my body, and then the one I was required to live. The latter was little more than a pretence, a necessary fabrication that enabled me to operate in my secret hive as I pleased. I had been playing a juggling game for weeks now, since I had finished the milkshakes and I was getting better at it. Of course there had been slip-ups. There were times when I simply couldn't find a way out of eating but I was reassured each time that tomorrow would be better. At first, she was soothing in this way. Every time I steered off-track, she would scorn me most severely with stringent words and undesirable truths before finally comforting me, telling me that every mistake would only accelerate me forward in my ambitions. More importantly, I started to understand that her somewhat brutal manner and verbal persuasion were crucial to our goals. It was as if I needed to be stripped of everything I had been before then. If she could break me down enough, then I would have no choice but to do everything she wished of me. If you make anyone – even yourself – feel bad enough about what they are, they will undoubtedly attempt to remedy the situation and 'fix' themselves. This was the doctrine she and I worked under for the duration of our relationship.

But wait a moment. What sane person would agree to such terms? Firstly, I don't think I was particularly sane or of the right mind at the time anyway. And secondly, she made it easy to commit to her. I have felt alone most of my life. Please don't misunderstand me; I come from a supportive family, have some of the closest friends one could be graced with and have seen boyfriends come and go over the years. And yet for all this, I have rarely felt truly connected with another person. Typical of any contemporary teenager, I have never belonged anywhere with much ease or comfort and thus have lived most of my young life in a rather lonely state. So when the occasion arose, I discovered that I was more than willing to give everything to this person I had created in my mind.

Though I'm sure it is entirely strange to take an illness such as bulimia nervosa and personify it to the extent I have over the years, doing so provided me with a friend like no other. She understood all that I was and appeared to know everything I would ever be. She saw every beam of light and every hidden shadow of who I was. What's more, she loved me anyway. And as my dependency on her existence manifested, so hers did to me. I didn't just need her; she needed me and the bond was impenetrable. I first heard of 'suicide pacts' when I was child. I learned how people, often strangers, would reach out for others who felt as sad as they did and how, from there, they would agree to kill themselves at the same time, as if it would take them away together and they wouldn't technically have to be alone. I didn't want to be alone anymore. While I didn't want to die, I probably would have if I thought I would lose her. But that's all rather heavy right now and not something I like to think about.

I make no attempts whatsoever to glorify bulimia, but I ultimately succumbed to my illness because I wanted to. I did not consciously agree to the repercussions it would bring, yet I subconsciously immersed myself into the darkest corners of my mind before finally, I just let go. The sensation was freeing. You see people like me don't just 'let go'. Since childhood, I held on so tightly to myself that now I often wonder how I could even breathe for all those years. Nevertheless I was convinced that if I let anything go, even for a moment, my world would crash and burn around me.

I AM NINE YEARS old. My sister Natalie and our friend Maeve play together every day. Maeve is more Natalie's friend than mine but they let me tag along because nobody else will play with me. We each have our own place in our group of three. Natalie is the leader because she's the oldest and the best at everything we do. We play whatever game she wants to play and do everything she says. I don't mind because I like to play with Natalie and Maeve, otherwise I'd be by myself.

Maeve is the funny one in our little group. She is Natalie's best friend and gets second pick of everything. She makes Natalie laugh and so I laugh too. I never play with Maeve when Natalie isn't here. When we first moved to our new house four years ago, Maeve's mum told her that she had to play with me. On my first day here, we went into the shed in our back-garden where all the toys are. Most of them were Natalie's and I wasn't allowed play with them. I was showing Maeve and another girl some of our toys and reached for one I liked most. When I turned around, the girls had run away. But now I see Maeve all the time because she likes Natalie.

It's dark outside so we have to play in the house. We're in our kitchen, which is very small but we like it because the grown-ups can't see us and we can do whatever we want. One of our favourite games is a racing one. Maeve and I are given a glass of water and a slice of bread each from Natalie. When Natalie shouts 'Go!' we must eat and drink as fast as we can and the first person to finish their bread and water wins. I don't really like this game because it makes me feel sick and I usually never win anyway. We've been playing it all night now and Natalie has been putting horrible-tasting things on our bread to make it more fun. But it's not all that fun; I drank so much water that I have a cramp in my stomach. My sides feel as though they've been injected with steel and every time I move, they're digging at my body. But there's very little I can do right now. When I play with Natalie, I always have to be very careful about what I say, do and what I show. If I step out of line in any way, she will either scorn me and I try to reduce her ammunition by never losing my myself in the moment and never allowing myself to slip up too badly. When we play together it's as if I'm clutching a stress ball in my hand. I squeeze it as tight as I possibly can and never let it go. I can't let it go. I can't drop it. If I do, my life will be hell and we both know it.

We've started playing Twister instead, where we use a coloured sheet and have to place a hand or foot on the given circle that Natalie calls out.

'Right-hand to red,' Natalie tells Maeve.

'Left-foot on blue,' she informs me. It continues like this for some time before I start to feel really sick. I'm bent over Maeve and our limbs are now awkwardly entwined on the coloured sheet.

'I have to go to the toilet,' I say in desperation.

'Not yet,' Natalie spits. 'We have to finish this round first.'

'But I really have to go.'

'Not yet!' she says again. But I can't hold it in any longer. I give up and pretend to fall over, forfeiting the round to Maeve. Natalie knows I've done it on purpose and is not happy with me. I run to the bathroom and knock on the door.

'I'll be out in a minute,' my Dad calls. I groan in urgency as I bob from one foot to the other in the hallway. Natalie and Maeve have appeared at the kitchen door and are laughing at me as I dance around the floor. The wait seems to last longer than it should and I can feel my panic and anxiety growing. I'm aware of my whole body now and have stiffened up so tight that my muscles are throbbing. I'm looking at Natalie and Maeve when I hear the bathroom door creak. There is a second noise behind me and in the moment I start to rotate, I see Natalie's face light up like a cat about to pounce on an unsuspecting bird.

'Leanne, come HERE!' she shouts in a frenzied voice. It takes only seconds but in those passing moments, everything slows and I can't help but walk toward her as she gestures me. I let that ball in my hand go and ignore the unlatching door behind me. The moment I reach my sister, her face changes and contorts itself into a smile, followed by roaring laughter. I hear darting feet on the floor behind me and veer around to see my older brother sprinting past my father and into the bathroom. As Dad shuffles away rather confused, I run to the door and begin screaming and banging on it.

'Mum!' I call. As Natalie and Maeve cry with laughter, I burst into tears of total panic and desolation. I am screaming at myself in my own head. I let the ball drop. That ball that kept me composed and in one piece was all I ever had to keep myself and I let it drop. Mum comes rushing out asking what's wrong, only to see me still hopping around outside the door.

'Peter, get out of the bathroom. Leanne needs to use the toilet now' she yells at my brother. But it's too late. My body has gone weak and limp. I feel the shame and degradation creep up my face, sizzling now with the heat of the moment. My legs are numb except for one feeling; the sensation of hot liquid running to my feet and my toes, burning into my skin as it goes. The bathroom door unlatches and the moment has passed. I stand in my spot calmly. I am lifeless and suddenly very small.

'Oh my God!' Natalie screeches. 'Look Maeve! She wet herself!' The two erupt uncontrollably and proceed to fall onto the floor, clutching each other in their fit. They were only young girls joking and messing about, but it had a huge impact on me. My brother pulls an awkward facial expression but can't help having to suppress a laugh before going into his room. Mum merely sighs; she must pity me so much and now she has to clean the hallway.

'Go and get changed Leanne' she says gently. Deflated and drained, I walk into my bedroom. My trousers are damp and ice cold now and I wish the ground would open up and consume me. I dropped the ball, I think to myself. I dropped that bloody ball.

It had been almost two months of on-off fasting before I really started to notice changes in my body. If I still carried that proverbial stress ball in my hand, I still clutched it as tightly as ever. The slim physique was of course the most evident change. Whereas before I had always justified my unbearable reflection with the usual intentions of bettering myself, I now enjoyed the pleasure of uncompromising reassurance. For every failure noted, I now had the tools and power to change anything I wanted. My chest no longer felt fraught under the weight of an iron clad and my body seemed to move in the same rhythm as my thoughts. It was as if all the weight had been shifted from my body and into my head. When my limbs moved, they felt loose and unrestricted. For every fibre that unwound itself under my skin, a cerebral knot tightened somewhere in my mind; it secured itself and locked in the given loss, as if in a feeding frenzy. The sensation experienced by my body as I continued to lose weight nourished the fattening demons that blockaded my head. Strange things started going missing.

First, it was the crease that fell mid-way up my back. Somewhere near the base of my ribcage and hovering not too far north of my hips, there once lay a modest crease. It reminded me of the brushwork of Renaissance painters who sought to capture the quiet beauty of the feminine form. But the crease went missing in those months and left behind only the faintest hint of its past existence. Along with it went the sallow strip of flesh that ran so smoothly over my knee caps. It was replaced instead with a seemingly irregular scattering of bone protrusions and cobbled surfaces. I also lost some of my smile. My laughter no longer managed to reach the folds around my mouth and the wrinkles that ran from my nose and down my cheeks could not cement themselves into my face as they had done before.

For everything we lose, however, we usually gain something else for better or worse. I grew bones I did not know were there. From my toes to my ankles, five solid strings attached themselves and resembled a spider's web up my foot. My stomach almost fell inwards and was concave in comparison to my ribs, which had apparently grown in size quite substantially. In bed at night, I would place the palms of my hands firmly against the broadest space taken up by those ribs. The skin that concealed them clung to their wave-like structure for dear life. It strapped itself around them and under my hand, I felt them rise and fall beneath the thin sheet of vellum. With every breath, my stomach disappeared further beneath my ribs and they slid against my interior walls like a snake on the sand.

I was suddenly more aware of my bones than I had ever been before this point. Mostly, this was due to the fact that they seemed to ache very often. By now, the disease of my mind had abandoned its roots in the corners of my skull and infested its way to the marrow of my bones. She wanted me to feel her everywhere and now my entire body knew about her presence. I didn't sit in one position for very long at any given time; my back would weigh down on the bones beneath it until I was so uncomfortable I'd have to assume a different position. At night, my knees would rub against one another like chalk on a blackboard and I slept with a pillow between them for fear they would wear away.

My skin, once soft and smooth around every turn, looked aged. It looked like every cigarette I had ever inhaled began to exhale back onto my exterior canvas. It wafted out of every pore and left a dry and haggard ash-stain in its path. My lips paled and my face lengthened uncomfortably. As dark circles formed an encasement from my brow to my cheeks, my eyes faded in tenacity and indeed, lost any if not all indication of the life behind them. Somewhere in those months, I think I slipped away beneath them. Hiding beneath whatever I could in order to shield myself was something I was always good at. Slipping under the radar was my forte and I enjoyed the protection it provided.

I AM 17 YEARS old. After two fleeting years, Stephen and I broke up only days ago. I think I knew that it had been coming for a while and just didn't want to believe it. I'm about to go to a birthday party and am sick to my stomach. The source of my upset is not that I miss

Stephen. Surprisingly, it's not as bad as I thought it would be. No, the main reason for my being so melancholy is because I miss the person I was when with him. After so long of being with someone, it's as if I became that person's interpretation of me. Everything I was could be wrapped up in what Stephen alone saw in me. He was like a safeguard, hiding me from everything I was afraid of. Now, I have nothing to hide behind and no radar to slip under and lie low.

Walking through my friend's house, I try my best to move like a shadow. I don't want to be noticed for fear of someone seeing that I'm missing a vital limb or something else of great importance. The crowd is an unfamiliar one with faces I've only ever seen once or twice. I try not to catch anyone's eye. I don't want them to look at me because I know they will observe how completely lost I am here. Instead, I retreat to the back of my encircled friends seeking solace and comfort.

'Have your eye on anyone, Leanne?' Kate smirks at me.

'No, I'm only looking. Don't think I could even if I wanted to.' As it turns out, this is a lie. Under particular circumstances, it's so easy so convince ourselves of what we're feeling rather than face the repercussions of the truth. The truth, in this instance, is that I do want to and there are one or two boys at the party who I have noticed very briefly. But I can't tell my friends this. If I do, a fuss will be made and a series of Chinese whispers will commence much the same as there would have been when I was 14. I can't take that kind of glossed-over mortification, let alone the pressure of it all.

Thankfully, this doesn't need to occur. In little to no time at all,

I'm talking to a local boy named Adam. Confident and outlandish, he's making this conversation easy for both of us. It's a weight off my shoulders. If nothing else, I know now that I can at least still talk to a member of the opposite sex without feeling utterly foolish. Moreover, I'm in shock that anyone would be interested enough to talk to me for this long. The conversation is typical and wonderful. From school to what we will go on to study and a few brief words on the party, the small talk was all I wanted and needed that night.

I'd had no intention of this night amounting to anything. At best, I wanted simply to come here this evening, trudge through it and go home where I can continue in my growing loneliness. And yet, this is not the case. As I talk with Adam, I'm bubbling over beneath the surface and surprised with myself. Not only am I very attracted to him, but it's as if his confidence has radiated to my very core. In his presence, a certain ease has descended over me and my worries of before have almost completely vanished. In this moment, I don't want to hide or disappear. Rather, I want to showcase myself and push this debutante feeling to its full potential.

'Here,' Adam says, taking my hand, 'let's go somewhere more private.' When we finally kiss, it's as if Stephen and the person I was with him, never existed. Beneath the uncertainty with which I walked in this evening, I must have been merely waiting for something to open a bolted door. Now open, I feel confident, attractive and what's more, I feel sure of the person under my own skin. I don't want to hide anymore and I can only hope this feeling lasts for ever.

AT A TIME WHEN everything about me seemed to go missing, it was difficult for me to remember moments when I stood alone and fully formed in my own head. Before that night, I hid extremely well under the covering shield of a boyfriend. With the realisation that this protection was gone, I knew then that I had to find some other means of guarding myself. As it turned out, the next thing or person I would hide beneath would be my bulimia.

I had lost a tremendous amount of weight, the figure I struggle to remember exactly. It was enough, however, for others to commence with their anticipated comments, some positive and some of less so. Being around people I hardly knew and had little regard for became the highlight of my declining social life. My closest friends, the people I had known and trusted for years and who knew me better than I cared to believe, became unbearable company. Their shrewd eyes were inescapable and insufferable. Our history together and all they knew of me became overwhelming. I couldn't breathe around them anymore. In the dead heat of their knowledge, it was stifling and completely suffocating. For the time being, I was done with them and all they had to offer. Instead, I felt at ease amongst strangers. I was comforted by how little they cared for me, as it guaranteed my own freedom among them; I didn't have to work as hard hiding the truth because with these people, the fabrication was enough and easily maintained. When I ventured as far as my local pub with friends, it wasn't long before I would abandon them and find a less challenging clique.

In this way, I eventually became defined by pretence, or at least I did in public. Self-definition was something I always strived for. I suppose I needed it. As a child, if I didn't define myself under particular headings then I would have been nothing at all, or so it seemed. Whereas I once classed myself as an academic and a master of intellectual advancement, I now wore the mask of the perfect socialite. In public, my facade was affecting and almost flawless. How I spoke, behaved and carried myself became everything I was. It sounds like a rather hollow existence and if that was everything I embodied then of course it would have been. But my life, under my logic of the time, was extremely fulfilling. I told myself I had everything a person should have and more.

The impeccable illusion experienced by others was only a facet of the person displaying it. Unlike the moronic primates I found in new companions, I possessed something more substantial. I felt superior to their insignificant cares because I just knew that they did not have the mental or even emotional capacity to understand me or even fully understand themselves. They lived a one-track life that was directed aimlessly under one mentality. I, on the other hand, functioned under a dual-ability to live as both the person she wanted me to be and the person they all wanted me to be. Therefore, I was safe in my belief that their superficiality could surely never contend with my own complexity. She convinced me of this and as such, made my one-woman show a triumphant success for a time.

Her presence in my life and in my personal development made everything possible. Of course, I had no way of knowing who or what she was back then but I was moderately insightful enough to know that there was something different about me, even if I couldn't put my finger on it. On a surface level, I just didn't question it. Whatever it was, it made my life easier and more manageable. But let's be realistic about this. I knew then as I know now, along with the rest of the human race, that a person should eat to live. My logic was not so forgiving in that sense and it obviously did not escape my attention that it wasn't normal to live as I was attempting to. I must have known this or else I wouldn't have been so desperate to conceal this secret life of mine.

Along with this, I was not so foolish to believe that everyone else lived and worked in the pain and discomfort that had become the norm for me. All memory of how my body should feel had disappeared. I was in a constant state of discomfort, to put it lightly. What most recognise as hunger pains were now excruciating and one of the only sensations I physically felt anymore. It felt like I was eroding from the inside out. Someone had carved a hole in my stomach and filled it with air. Eating steadily changed from something I would prefer to avoid doing to an unimaginable act of weakness. There were days I was convinced if I put anything into my mouth, I would feel it moving through me like an alien intruder that my body was trying to resist. I would feel it at the back of my mouth, chewed and fully-prepped to launch an aggressive assault. I would feel it creeping down my throat, building momentum and stealth. More than anything else, I would feel it grounded to the bottom of my once divinely empty stomach, rotting and stewing. It would begin an assault from that advantageous position and infest its way into my bloodstream, my defenceless cells and the bodily walls that shielded and protected it from being ripped out immediately. It was using my own body against me and as a result, it became all too easy for my mind to register that food was the enemy.

The most powerful weapon against it was, quite simply, prevention. Once in my stomach, there were limited cures and the only degree of safety to be upheld was through enduring resistance. I would not do that to myself; she wouldn't let me, she cared too much. So I would not eat and that was final.

Through such justifications, it gradually became easier and easier to suppress the hunger pains and even tolerate the stabbing intensity of a truly empty stomach. I soon found myself enjoying the pain: It would spark in the lowest point of my stomach, light like a match and blaze until I thrashed in flames. Then it would tear north, shredding my sides and scorching beneath the skin that enveloped my chest. It was more than hunger. My insides screamed at a deafening pitch, unable to fight the devouring emptiness. Soon it was like my body turned against me in desperation. The hollow sting that I nurtured so affectionately began to eat away at me instead. It fed off my muscles and biological insulation. I thought it a most fair trade. The person who lived in my head was the most important priority now. If she was the predator, I was happy for my body to be the prey. I would permit her to feed until fully cultivated. In doing this, I knew I could finally satisfy that impossible hunger which had gripped me so many months before.

Anything I had to give in return for this seemed insignificant; whatever it was, it would be a small sacrifice by comparison. One forfeit made, for example, was bodily. I'm sure that must sound very strange but constantly being cold was something I had to adjust to rather quickly. With little or no nutrition to thrive on, my body temperature dropped rapidly. It wasn't the same as getting a draught from an open window; the cold had seeped into my bones and stayed there like an anchor on the seabed. It would not be moved and I would feel almost no warmth whatsoever. My hands and feet felt it the most. While no amount of layering could ease the piercing ice that ate at my toes, my fingers couldn't feel to grip anymore. It had become too painful for my hands to do most things that others surely take for granted as I did before. From making a cup of tea, to dialling a number on the telephone and even trying to write, my hands felt like they were cramping up and just couldn't work with quite the same efficiency.

The worst memory I have of being extremely cold was at a friend's birthday party. It was August and given the fortunate weather of late, said companion resolved to throw a barbecue in her garden to celebrate. It had been only a few hours since the party began when shadows started chasing one another on the ground and the sun was remembered only through the amber and pink remnants imprinted in the sky. Darkness fell and with it, the heat of the sun vanished. Heaters and garden lights dotted the gathering of people and I gravitated toward them, unable to focus on much else. As always, I tried my best to stay perfectly in sync with the chorus of conversation around me. Part of being perfect was to always appear so and with this ideal in mind, I thought it best to simply ignore the distraction of my numb fingers and toes. I laughed and smiled, playing my part faultlessly and still managing to avoid the food passing from plate to plate. But my skin prickled so much that it began to sting. My feet may as well have detached themselves from my body and taken a walk elsewhere, while my nose was about to crumble and turn inwards into my face.

'Jesus!' someone choked beside me. 'Leanne, you're lips are blue! Are you cold?' I laughed it off uncertainly before making a swift exit from the situation and to the nearest bathroom. When I looked in the mirror, it took a moment to fully appreciate what exactly was looking back at me. Yes, my lips had gone a faded shade of blue-gray and seemed to jump out from my face, which had turned a deathly white. I looked like a porcelain doll, I thought, except for the flawless finish. I had put my make-up on immaculately that evening, leaving no room for mistakes or blemishes anywhere. And yet, something looked different about my face. Something was wrong with it. Aside from the very obvious bizarreness of my blue lips, my complexion was gaunt and hallowed. It reminded me of a cracked painting, damaged through the years of wear and tear. Though you saw no out-of-place contour from my forehead to my chin, the overall composure was ghostly. It wasn't my face. I stared at my own reflection, convinced that there was someone else in the room with me.

I was so suddenly stricken with panic. My hands had been shaky and uneasy for as long as I could remember, but now they trembled violently along with the rest of my body. My knees clattered against one another and my pores began to release cold perspiration. Finally, my throat started to close up and I couldn't breathe. Something terrible was about to happen, I was sure of it. With that one fleeting thought, I was mentally committed to the notion that there was no escaping this horrible event that was about to unfold. It could have been anything; the bathroom door was jammed and I was about to faint with claustrophobia or the roof was about to fall in on me. Someone in the garden was about to fall and hit their head because I left my bag thrown on the ground or someone was about to burst in and accuse me of not eating. It didn't matter what it was. For some reason, in that moment, I was doomed and the reality of this brought me to the floor. I was nauseous, my head was spinning and I wanted to get as close to the ground as possible. I curled up in a foetal position on the tiles; cold, shaking and dizzy. It was as if I was watching myself from the eyes of a third person. I witnessed everything a split-second after

I did it. I saw myself get up, pace momentarily and eventually wrap my arms around my knees on the bathroom tiles. I would have cried but the anxiety had paralysed my body. I couldn't catch my breath long enough to even do so. Without a doubt, I was definitely going to vomit. I closed my eyes for what felt like the longest time until finally, the ominous cloud lifted and I was back in my body and lying on a bathroom floor. The same song that had been playing outside when I first came into the bathroom was still playing now, thumping through the walls. Only minutes had passed.

I eventually stood up – albeit too quickly – and endured the last momentary blinding of my own light-headedness before I was at long last, looking at myself in the mirror again. It still wasn't me and if anything, the reflection looked worse now than it had a few moments ago. I splashed water on the back of my neck, which made my already freezing fingers throb. After fumbling for some tissue, I dabbed my face gently and took off the glossy shine that now ruined my previously spotless make-up. It was no use and I was too cold anyway. That panicked feeling in the pit of my stomach had not fully retreated and for fear of it surfacing again, I was quick to grab my things, give my apologies to the hostess and leave as soon as I could. In bed that night, I could finally breathe properly once more.

More than anything else, I was physically exhausted and may as well have just run a marathon. I didn't even care about how cold I was. My body had never felt so small or so fragile. In one sense, it was a moment of ecstasy and I was comforted with soft, almost compassionate, encouragement.

Delicate, she said. The word imprinted on me like the cold before it. I was weak and going numb, but I was delicate. This is what I had wanted. I wanted to lose weight and retain some ounce of delicacy to resemble that of the spider-figured women I had seen in all those flashing images. Suddenly, the lack of strength displayed by my body was counterbalanced with a surging lease of mental satisfaction and might. As I lay in bed, buried under all my layers of clothes and bed sheets, the warmth still could not reach me. It was too late for that now and I didn't care. I just wanted to sleep, basking in my success and enduring the cold until I could finally slip into a forgetful slumber.

Naturally, I tried to combat the freezing temperatures of my body with excessive clothing and found myself wrapped in layer upon layer, looking rather strange most of the time at home. It also served a dual purpose. Beneath the heavy folds, my body was free to waste away without too much attention. I have always been big-boned – the old cliché – my mother used it to reassure me as a child that this was why I looked bigger than the other kids. She was right to a certain extent. I did have a rather broad frame. It was being shaped liked this that allowed me to get away with the weight loss I experienced. Beneath my baggy clothes, my frame didn't appear all that different to what it was before. The body that was hidden under these clothes was mine. Eventually, that body would go numb and devoid of all feeling. Soon after, all I began to feel was my brain pulsing between my eyes. With less and less of my body to be seen as time passed, my head became everything I was and all I lived. While I owned my body, my head owned me and somewhere in my consciousness, I accepted it most apathetically.

Though psychologically I felt liberated and powerful while fasting, my mind was of course split in two ways on the matter. On the one hand, I was merely doing what had started to feel natural to me – or at least what I had convinced myself was natural to me. On the other, it is impossible to fully ignore basic urges, no matter how well you have trained your brain. Consequently, I was haunted by food. While my body continued on its degenerative path, my senses seemed to explode from time to time. Particularly my sense of smell. Of course I would not eat whatever food was before me, but smelling it was something entirely different. I started smelling everything. Cooked meals always smelled the most potent and would travel from a hot pan straight to my nose, filling me and testing me. Salty foods would tickle my nostrils; nuts, crisps and popcorn were the main culprits. Such processed foods were packed to full capacity with salty gusto and aromas.

Above anything else, however, fruit would tempt me endlessly. I can sense your bewilderment now. Of all foods, why would someone be most tempted by fruit? I asked myself the same question. My house is and always has been one of full cupboards. My mother's sweet tooth meant that our kitchen was bursting at the seams with treats and chocolate. Despite this, I showed little interest in these things while fasting. I considered once that maybe I didn't crave these foods because of their availability. We each want what we can't have, after all. The problem with this theory is that technically nothing was available to me anymore and there was no reason why my mouth should water at the sight of a fruit bowl and not an open box of chocolates. What made me so desperate for my mother's fruit bowl, which was always full, was the natural goodness I knew it had. It was as if my body, after so long without proper nutrition, craved natural excellence only.

The smell of fruit was more tantalizing because my body knew it would service it better than anything else. The smell of that fruit bowl screamed of hydration and physical restitution. It also teased my very eyes. I had never noticed before how vibrant the colours were in a fruit bowl. The combination of sight and smell left me ravenous for that fruit. I thought so often of Eve in the Garden of Eden and even fancied myself a modern equivalent. Eve must have been bulimic, I once joked. Nothing could have tempted her more than the sight and smell of that apple and I thought that had I been in her position, I would have tossed eternal life and happiness out the window for just one bite.

Poor woman, I thought. *Of course the will against temptation had to fall on her. She never had a chance.*

Being surrounded by food became a strange and almost sadistic pleasure for me. While it tortured that part of me that still wanted to live as I had for so many years, I couldn't stay away from those smells. It made me strong too. Every moment spent around food tested my ability to resist it. When I did so, she fired up inside me like a revved engine. Her vigour and unheralded zeal in those moments was a compelling sensation and I soaked it all in. Of course, there was only a very fine line that wavered between smelling the food and actually eating it; one slip-up and I knew I could lose complete control of myself. I stayed focused and headstrong on the matter.

Smoking helped. It would curb the hunger pains and provided the entertainment that was now missing due to the absence of food in my life. More than just something to do with my hands, I found myself tricked into believing one could survive on cigarettes, water and black coffee if they needed to. And I did.

Over time, fasting became my natural way of living from day to day. I struggled to remember how I could have ever lived any other way but this. The mind can condition the body to do anything. Our bodies are at the mercy of our own mentality. It's when the problem is in the mind in the first place that the real trouble starts. Although extreme and dangerous, my illness was never about my actions. They were mere manifestations of something bigger. It was about the mind that guided them and the technical faults in its ability to do so. Under this theory an eating disorder is a mentality, albeit an unhealthy one. It is a way of thinking that dictates our life and how we choose to live it. Through the mentality of bulimia or any other illness, the world and our place in it are seen completely differently, as if a new shade has been cast over their original appearance. Through my mentality of the time, everything in the world was seen through a bulimic light.

Bulimia nervosa is a cyclic lifestyle and consists of three main stages, which are repeated over and over. Unaware of the trap I had by now fallen into very deeply, I was in the first stage of bulimia. The behaviours of a bulimic may be documented in their reoccurring fasting, bingeing and purging. For me, this cycle was daily and sometimes even hourly. But looking back, the trend dominated those two years in a much broader way too. I had been fasting on and off for months before I ever considered purging. But after so long without eating – or even just eating properly – I found myself in an uncontrollable state, which had to be remedied. Purging would become an intricate part of my life but I would reach rock bottom before finally getting to that point.

THE BINGE

I'M UNSURE OF MY age. I look relatively older, maybe 18, but feel as small as a six-year-old. I can't be certain. I'm alone and surrounded by tables of food, displayed beautifully and just begging to be eaten. I know I shouldn't eat anything; if I do, I will ruin all my hard work thus far and then I will balloon in size. Instead, I just smell the food for a while. As I breathe in, I move my mouth in a chewing motion, pretending that I'm eating that delicious odour; this way, I can persuade myself into believing that I'm inhaling the food itself.

Everyone wants me to eat. My friends, my family, sometimes even those vague faces I drink with are all nitpicking at me below the surface, willing me to feed myself. I know that they can see I haven't been eating anything and they're all just itching to say something. My family would just love if I kept eating; I would stay they're fat little girl for ever, exactly how they want me. And why would my friends want me to stop eating? We're each in one big competition after all, contending with one another to look the best and to be the most attractive. They would never admit to it but I know this to be the case.

I won't lose. I've lost too many times before. I'm going to win, I think to myself.

Yet for all my reasoning and determination, I can't stop looking at this beautiful food in front of me with my mouth watering up. The very air that surrounds me has been polluted with the allurement of this food, wrapping itself around my flaccid body, beguiling all my unsophisticated senses. If only there was some way of eating it and then making it disappear. Maybe I could invent a time machine that would allow me eat the food, fondly remember the sensation of doing so and later return to the moment before I put anything in my mouth and stop. Sometimes I do miss eating the way other people do. But I'm convinced now that all is not what it seems.

When I see a very thin girl mindlessly scoffing her meal at a restaurant, I think to myself, *That must be the first meal she has eaten in months*; because it's just not possible for anybody to eat in this supposedly 'normal' fashion and still remain that skinny. If this is the case, then my contention that I am a freak is correct. Not only do I function under an evidently eccentric mentality by comparison, but even my body cannot operate as others do because unlike these bodies, mine simply can't absorb food without erupting at the seams of my waistline.

Despite this knowledge, I start to give in to all those pressing temptations. I dive into the spread before me, hoping that if I chew loudly it will drown out the screaming voice in my head. It's too late for her to stop me now anyway; a few bites and I've already ruined myself so I may as well commit fully to my sin. I'm eating only a very short while before I start to get pains in my stomach. I knew this was a bad idea and suddenly I can no longer drown out that screaming in my head; it's all I can hear or feel now. I finally stop and realise that I'm lighted-headed, as if I've been pumped with hot air and the only thing holding me to the ground is this gall at the base of my torso.

I fall back into bed, where I'm almost certain I came from in the first place. Everything has gotten a bit blurry now. I've lost track of time and it's dark outside so I can't see anything properly. I wipe my mouth where a bit of drool had been trickling down and am suddenly aware that something isn't right. Grabbing a nearby hand-mirror, I can just about make out my face in a ray of light, the source of which I do not know. As if an apocalypse has decided to take place in my head, all horrors of the world seem to crash down on top of me, igniting trepidation and hysteria. All my teeth have fallen out. I open my mouth just wide enough to see big pink gums and my tongue falling around in my mouth, no teeth to keep it fenced in.

'Mum!' I start screaming, but to little avail because it sounds too muffled for anyone to hear. 'Mum! Come in here, Mum! My teeth, I need help!'

When I finally woke up, I was temporarily still convinced that there wasn't a tooth left in my head. After a few moments of lingering distress, I slumped back on my pillow, reassured that it had just been a dream. But my uneasiness was always difficult to shake off and these nightmares usually left a moody and irritable residue to each new day's premiere. They were quite common by that point in my life. Perhaps they had even become nightly occurrence but thankfully I didn't always remember them. They were more or less the same from night to night; I would start bingeing on food in whatever the given circumstance and would somehow finish the dream with no teeth and an alarmingly realistic foreboding that would persist long after waking.

They were only dreams and given I had never read too deeply into them in the past I wasn't about to start doing so now, regardless of the context. Besides, I had little interest in dwelling upon the subconscious when my conscious reality had begun to reach such a point of turmoil. An eating disorder comes about as a consequence of a great number of varying factors, as we have seen and continue to explore. What enables it to persevere and adopt new manifestations is often subject to the ongoing lifestyle of the given individual. As well as feeding on the person whose body it inhabits, an eating disorder feeds on the environment in which it lives. It is mutable in this way. Its ability to bend and contort as a means of fitting the necessary mould is both skilful and an absolute requirement to guarantee its further existence.

I suppose, it is this faculty that determined my eating disorder as bulimia as opposed to anything else. It took a measure of time though; I suffered an eating disorder long before I acted out any bulimic behaviours. The problem is that these words, phrases and concepts to which we attribute such mental illnesses are too ambiguous in their meaning. They are umbrella terms that have been generalised to a point of mild obscurity, if not total equivocation. Moreover, our understanding of them is usually very primitive, perhaps even completely ignorant, in comparison to the complexity of the particular disease. An acquaintance of mine, with whom intellect had not graced and who was aware that I'd struggled in this way, once highlighted my point perfectly.

'Aren't you, like, anorexic or something?' he said to me. Yes, he executed his question exactly like that. Needless to say, I was unimpressed. But there seemed little point in lying; I had only recently written an article for my university newspaper in which I detailed my story, hoping to God some good may come out of it. Instead, I got this guy.

'No. I'm bulimic' I told him.

'Oh right, yeah. That's the one where you make yourself sick, isn't it?'

'That's the one.' If monotone sarcasm ever had a moment of prodigious notoriety, that would have been it. *Well this is just brilliant*, I thought to myself. Two years of emotional and psychological depravity and in one sentence, this guy had defined what it is to be a bulimic, convinced himself of whatever meaning he gave it and I imagine that in his own head, the matter was now completely resolved and closed for ever.

If I worked under the terms that this person set down for bulimia, for example, then what was I before I began purging? I don't think it is so simple that I could say I was anorexic for some months and then later turned bulimic. Perhaps it would make all this much easier for us to comprehend if we opted to believe the above. But in doing so, we would disregard the accuracy with which we are attempting to analyse an eating disorder. Sometimes I wonder if it's possible to be bulimic without displaying bulimic behaviours such as purging. But then I realise that nobody would understand this, not without understanding her and how she conducts herself. The fasting process I underwent prior to my bulimia was, you see, part of it. It was key in the cyclical behaviours that are governed by a repetitive mentality. One doesn't merely resolve to never again let a meal rest in their body. Something has to provoke the thought and more than this, something has to make you really believe it.

In this way, my months of fasting didn't merely provide me with the determination to just lose weight; they instilled that raw and pure belief in what I was doing. Though others may argue that the overall purpose was to lose weight, in reality, purpose had very little to do with it. Belief is a staggeringly powerful weapon and once it existed in its truest form, I abandoned logic because I knew that it could be championed by blind faith anyway. This was how I ought to live and I believed that, for the sake of believing something.

I've been told I have an addictive personality. It's a fair assertion and not something I would deny with too much haste. I'm susceptible to becoming addicted to most things; lifestyles, people, moods, activities, you name it. It's this aspect to my character that often sanctions and fuels my perfectionism in life. But through all my time spent thinking over those two years, I have wondered so much whether I simply allowed myself to become addicted to that bulimic mentality. Or better still, perhaps I just became addicted to the concept of belief, no matter where it fell. It's natural for everyone to want to believe in something. I've never been an exception; my belief in God, for example, has been unyielding and pure in substance. I've had blind faith in Him since an extremely young age, probably since I was old enough to even grasp the notion. I never remember a time in my life when God was not in it.

I AM SEVEN YEARS old. I attend family Mass every Sunday with Mum and Natalie. Dad and Peter don't go to mass anymore so I pray extra hard for them. I always link Mum's arm and Natalie does the same on the other side of her; we get uncomfortable on the wooden benches and fight with one another so Mum separates us by putting herself between us. But today Natalie and I can't fight because it's my First Holy Communion and everyone has to be on their best behaviour. Father Peter hasn't even started speaking yet but I'm already tired.

Last night, Mum put the rags in my hair to prepare me for today. While I was practising singing This Little Light of Mine, she shredded a towel into strips, curled each around a chunk of my hair and knotted it on my head. I hate the rags and usually cry because they hurt my head. My hair is full with ringlets of hair now and my scalp is still sizzling from when they were taken out this morning. I don't know why we spent so much time on my hair because it's covered with a veil now anyway. I'm wearing Natalie's Communion dress, which has been altered to fit me and also to look slightly different so nobody will know it's the same dress. It resembles a white wedding cake, with frills falling like snow atop its silk threading and a pink bow at every turn. But it still feels too tight because Natalie is smaller than me and I'm too fat for it. I move around awkwardly, my dress making a noise similar to paper scraping on the floor with every gesture.

I've been looking forward to today for a really long time. My teacher had everyone in the class make their own poster with a stained-glass candle. They're made out of coloured crepe paper, all stuck together on one sheet. Looking around, the church walls are dotted with those paper candles. Blues, reds, yellows and greens illuminate the building when hit by the rays of sunlight beating in. I've heard of the Northern Lights and how you can only see them in certain parts of the world. Spinning my head around all the colours of the church, I think this is like the crepe paper version of the Northern Lights. All the preparation we did was worth it because amidst the rainbow-spotted walls, I can see my stained-glass candle. It looks just as important as everyone else's and I feel part of something really big. My candle belongs on that wall the way I belong to Jesus and to God.

After the first hymn, Father Peter starts speaking up on the altar. He's my favourite priest in St. Fergal's Parish because he hasn't got grey hair yet, sings along with the choir and always talks to everyone after Mass. I've also never taken confession with him; I don't like seeing the priests after I've taken confession because then they know all the lies I've told, how often I fight with my sister and how sometimes I don't say my prayers. For now, Father Peter knows none of these things and I'm glad. When everyone is listening to the readings, I'm looking at the wooden crucifix that hangs at the top of the church. It's huge and always looks like it's about to fall down but after so long of seeing it, I never notice it anymore. It should scare me but it doesn't because there is at least one crucifix in every house I've been inside; I'm used to them. But for now, I'm lost in that crucifix at the top of the church, thinking about Jesus and whether he made a lot of money on his Communion day. Everyone says that relatives, like all your aunts and uncles, have to give you money when you make your Communion; some kids make hundreds.

But I don't want to make loads of money because it means that I have to spend the day visiting neighbours and relatives to collect it. I hate doing that because everyone will ask me stupid questions that they don't want to ask and that I don't want to answer. I'd prefer not to go visiting and just forget about the money. Besides, Ms Dilleen says that we're not supposed to hope for money or presents and that today is special because it is the first time we will receive the Holy Eucharist. If we wish for anything else, we shouldn't receive the Body of Christ because nothing is more important than that. I don't want to accept the Body for the wrong reasons because I want Jesus to trust me.

'You're lying.' Gerald said to me in class last week. 'Everybody wants money on their Communion. Stop lying.'

'I'm not lying.' I told him.

'Yes you are. You don't actually think God is real, do you?'

'He is real.'

'I bet you believe in Santa too.' Gerald laughed at me all day after that and told everybody that I believed in Santa Claus. I wanted to tell everyone that Gerald didn't believe in God because I know everybody does and that they would think he was really bold for not believing in Him. But I was afraid of getting in trouble with the teacher, so did nothing instead.

It doesn't matter what Gerald said anyway because it's a sin to not believe in God. I've been looking forward to my Communion for weeks and even though I know Gerald is probably really bored somewhere in the church, I'm too happy today to care. But when I finally receive the Holy Communion, the moment passes before I know it has happened. I thought when I first took the Body that it would be a moment of pure magic and that I would feel God's touch, like a spell had been cast on me. I barely realise it has even occurred until the wafer-thin bread gets stuck to the roof of my mouth as I walk back to my seat. I don't mind any of this because I know that God doesn't have to prove anything to me and that this is the whole point of belief and why they call it 'blind faith'. We were told this in school and so I believe it.

After what feels like an exceptionally long Mass, all my extended family and I make our way to the Fitzpatrick Castle Hotel in Killiney to enjoy a meal. But by the time we've gotten there, I feel like crying and want to go home. Mum and Dad are seated on either side of me in one of the big gardens; they want to have some photographs taken to remember the day, but I won't smile.

'Leanne, what's wrong?' Mum asks me. I refuse to answer and everyone is getting fed up with me.

What I don't want to tell her is that I'm not pretty enough for today and that I'm not sure Jesus wants to be my friend. I don't want to be here anymore. I want to take off my sister's dress, tear off my white veil and pretend I'm not here. But I can't tell her any of that because then I'd have to tell her about what happened after Mass. I'd have to tell her how Gerald stood beside me and told me, 'You shouldn't be here.'

'Why not?' I asked him

'Because nobody likes you and Jesus didn't have any ugly friends like you anyway. All his friends were pretty.'

'No, they weren't.' I told him uncertainly.

'Yes they were. So you shouldn't be here.' When Father Peter walked over, Gerald didn't say anything and neither did I.

Mum and Dad are getting really angry with me now because I don't want to be in any of the photographs. Eventually, they give up and we go back to the hotel for the big dinner. I'm not hungry anymore. I feel like I don't deserve to be Jesus' friend, but I hope that maybe he won't mind if I pray to him anyway.

THERE IS A NAIVETY among adults when it comes to children that they understand little and therefore, are perhaps limited in their ability to cause harm. I disagree. The capacity that children have to understand – albeit not fully – the things they do and various actions they take, is shockingly potent. Though I was never deterred from my faith by the cruel words of one boy, the dynamics of my relationship with God changed and, in truth, I don't know if I have ever felt worthy of His love. Moreover, I have been sure for years that He has never cared for, nor required my faith. Subject to my own character, however, I have been nevertheless dedicated and completely addicted to that belief in Him.

More than weekly Mass attendance and conventional bedtime prayers, my faith in Him is an internal flame that simply refuses to burn out. The institution of the Catholic Church, which I have followed my entire life, remains only the facility I utilize in guiding that flame. And if ever my confidence in the institution finds fault or wavers, I am at liberty to turn inwards and seek peace in that most inviolable and faithful niche within. This is the power of belief and once instilled in a person's definitive make-up, it lives with them in a most private manner.

Much like my devoted belief in God, the faith I had in my own illness was something I seemed addicted to. Understand me well when I say that I make absolutely no comparison between God and bulimia; but for a time in my life, both retained almost equal power over me and sometimes I wonder if I gave up on God in favour of my disease. The very thought upsets me and it's usually something I try not to think about. If I were to completely admit the unvarnished truth, I would probably say that for that time in my life, I felt like God wasn't enough and that my faith in Him simply couldn't make me as happy as my relationship with bulimia. Or else, I just didn't need Him as much as I thought I needed her. The sacrifices I made for her were, apparently, boundless.

While my reliance on her hit an all-time high and my devotion to God started stumbling, I found that my reclusive behaviour had become impossible. It had begun to draw too much attention among friends and family. Furthermore, from time to time, I would miss the life I used to enjoy. I had convinced myself that I had a greater purpose than others around me. While they luxuriated in social drinking, recreational activities and other simplistic fancies, I had surrendered to the darkness inside me. It had been, I thought, a necessary part of this greater purpose. But my pledge could only last so long. That's the problem with this stage of bulimia nervosa; it's usually only temporary because sooner or later, you just *have* to eat. I never considered that this lifestyle of fasting could last forever and for this reason, I have never believed myself to be anorexic. When you're anorexic I assume that this is the natural way of living and thinking, much the same way as bingeing and purging is to bulimia. But it was never my natural way, merely a temporary stepping-stone to the next place.

We have briefly touched upon the issue of bingeing, though not fully appreciated the significance of its place within bulimia. You see, a binge is almost always inevitable when one goes without eating for such a long period of time. It doesn't just satisfy the physical hunger that becomes you; it nourishes the psychological need to escape from your own controlling mind. In this way, the binge presents itself as the ultimate loss of control. It is the undesired pinnacle of a bulimic cycle and formed the collective moments of failure and shame that plagued me during that period. Bingeing was as common an occurrence as purging, given that if I hadn't binged I would have nothing to vomit up anyway. But before we address the idiosyncratic measures involved in bingeing, I feel it necessary to explain how I came to define eating from bingeing.

After months without proper food, I would say my body was near ready to give up completely. My muscles had deteriorated, my energy levels were run into the ground and most of the time I was in tremendous discomfort, if not exhausting pain. I had forgotten what it was to eat when it took my fancy and because it was no longer a regular daily routine, it was as if I had fallen out of practise. I didn't know how to eat anymore, not the way others did. It was too monumental an act now to just 'eat'. Here is where the distinction between eating and bingeing began to form and also where my aforementioned lack of moderation would prove to be most destructive. I suppose it developed largely due to the concept of proportion. When we're hungry, we eat in proportion to that hunger and pacify it adequately. But when you haven't eaten for so long, it's impossible to know how much food is required to fill that void which had taken up permanent residence in your stomach. And so, I didn't merely eat, as the very thought seemed outrageous under these circumstances. Instead, I binged. It was an entirely different act, as we will explore at a later stage.

Much the same way that I fasted for months, I underwent a period of time in which I binged in more ways than one. Looking back, I'd say it lasted for only about a handful of weeks. It felt like longer at the time. You would think that one would feel a sense of liberation but that wasn't the case. I had been so disciplined and perfectly controlled that sometimes I wonder if my subconscious was rebelling against the conscious mentally I lived under. Although that's probably impossible because my subconscious was usually the problem in these things and that more than anything else, I felt ashamed of how out of control I was for those weeks. It was more than just letting my weight go; I let go of that tight grip which held me for so long. It was like all the straps that fastened themselves round the cusps of my character suddenly buckled. The seams of who I was trying to be burst and I lost all sense of definition. Without that definition, so went moderation. I retained little purpose anymore and therefore allowed my once-rigorous direction to go askew.

I ate whatever I wanted and ignored the alarm bells that chimed over and over in my head. My previously burning mind iced over and I now worked neither for my body nor my mind. I was a loose cannon, exploding amidst the chaos of uncontrollable urges. During this period, my sense of taste burst open. It was reawakened in a most crude fashion and stronger than any drug addiction, once revived, I could not see past the hunger or the cravings any longer. I ate until my stomach throbbed several times on a daily basis. It seemed to please others around me and so I began to associate food with the concept of being watched. It was a show as well as everything else. I performed a daily matinee of meals and snacks in a manner more grotesque than I'm ready to admit to just yet. I would wait out the stomach pains, which often seemed worse than any hunger cramps I had known before. Eventually, I would slip under the overpowering thump of anguish and retire into what I came to call 'food comas'. Food, in the excessive way I consumed it, was paralysing and usually left me in so much discomfort that I was unable to function properly and would have to simply sleep it off.

Drinking also featured in my life in a way it never had before.

Alcohol was apparently more unavoidable than food and I remember many nights when, during my feeble attempts to regain control of myself, I would drink on an empty stomach. I would endure an entire day's worth without any food, telling myself that I was back on track, but would binge drink later in the night. Aside from the many health risks this lifestyle involved, I was usually conducting myself under one of two states. The first was total oblivion; I was either wiped out from the endless intake of food or else was smothered with the overwhelming inebriation of alcohol. The second was my own exhausted attempts at recovery from one or both of the above; I spent this time either sleeping through the food coma or the crippling hangover from the night before. This was my life for weeks and it seemed to please everyone just fine. As long as my family saw me eating and my friends saw me drinking socially, they were satisfied, unaware that my bingeing was just as dangerous and volatile as my fasting had been before it.

I recall a friend's birthday spent in our local pub. Ami was turning 19 and we celebrated first with a surprise birthday party, to which I played host, and later with drinks. It was a most horrific night, in which a major turning point came for me in my illness. The day had been another 'get back on the horse' kind and I had avoided food all day, promising myself that I wouldn't allow temptation to defeat me. One day at a time, I told myself, and I wouldn't permit my silly cravings or peer-pressure to interrupt the mighty pursuit at hand. Yet when the moment finally arrived, I disintegrated. All my discipline and all my promises came to nothing that night.

It started with a glass of white wine, which couldn't be avoided during a toast. 'It's just one glass,' I whispered to myself. But in truth, it's never just one glass or just one anything for that matter. That's the problem with myself and others of my age; we sacrifice well thought-out moderation for the extremities of experience, hoping that we may reap the fruits of our endeavours in one way or another. I've seen it with alcohol more than anything else. What we of my generation do to our bodies on a weekly basis through the consumption of alcohol is nothing short of mass destruction. Yet it is met with an air of acceptance, which enables our actions, if not condones them entirely. And so we are often limitless in how far we will push those boundaries. Natural of our age I suppose but still little justification. I made this mentality applicable to most facets of my life during what I now call my 'big binge' (big because it was the first and it incorporated so much over such a long period of time). Everything I did was carried out under that rather haphazardly extreme fashion and any potential consequences bore little relevance in making my decisions.

So when a second drink was passed into my hand the night of Ami's 19th birthday, I accepted effortlessly, having already failed my day and possessing little concern for any repercussions. Once I had failed, even moderately, then I would abandon redemption, simply committing to the bad deed I had already started. That is exactly what I did on this particular occasion. Binge drinking seems perfectly acceptable in contemporary culture. So when I declared, 'You know what? I think I'm just going to get wasted tonight,' it was met with a warm reception. I think I drank a bottle of white and devoured an unnerving amount of party food, including Brie and crackers, birthday cake, sandwiches and nuts. All mixed in my stomach not long before we were due to leave for the nightclub, I felt like I was on the verge of passing out with all the chemicals now hibernating in my system.

I felt extraordinarily exposed in that state, like my body wasn't my own. It didn't belong to me or my illness and instead tossed itself amidst the air of no man's land, a purgatory in which there lived no purpose or even hope. The safety I had found in fasting had all but disappeared and I was falling fast, nothing to grab on to, nobody to save me and no place to retreat to and call home. With it came those nerves that had haunted me since early childhood. It was as if I was unprotected, like eating and drinking ensured something horrific would transpire in this now strange place. I had no harbour in which I could find asylum and rode on a current too powerful to control. Getting into the taxi that night, I tried to shake those forgotten feelings but to little avail. They resurrected inside me at an alarming pace.

I AM 11 YEARS old. The trouble with the girls in school started a while ago but Mum doesn't know and now I can't sleep anymore. I remember having problems sleeping when I was very little. Just before bedtime, I would become so anxious that I would feel sick to my stomach and I often cried for fear of being away from my parents, even though they were just down the hallway. I have no idea why it started but being away from Mum became a matter of urgency and it's still an issue now. Since the girls at my school started being nasty to me, it's gotten a lot worse and when I lie in bed upstairs, I feel like I can't breathe because it's too warm. My mouth dries up with the growing temperature and sometimes I have to gasp for air. I know most kids don't like going to bed but this is different because I shake with terror when I have to go. I get so nervous when I'm alone up there. Mum tried leaving my bedroom door open and the landing light switched on, but it hasn't made a difference. I still feel that panic setting in, as I watch the sitting-room clock tick it's way to 9.00 pm, waiting for the drama to start unfolding.

Please stop, please stop, please stop, I pray in my head, wishing I could just stay up a little longer. I have become a nuisance to everyone in the house because bedtime is now a really horrible part of the day. I know everybody wants me to just go to bed and fall asleep like a normal kid but I just can't and now I get scared that I won't sleep, which keeps me awake even longer.

When I lie in bed, worrying that I will be awake forever, I think about bad things. I think about having to go to school tomorrow and suddenly I'm really upset. I can see myself getting up in the morning, putting on my school uniform, getting into the car and then being dropped off at the school gates. This sends shock waves through my body and I'm pumped with adrenaline, unable to focus on anything else but the thought of leaving this house tomorrow. Other times it's even worse and I think about my Aunt Susie's house. One Christmas, her house caught fire with Susie, her husband and their two children still inside it. It was Christmas Eve and their television, which was left plugged into the socket, sparked and caused the fire. The sitting room went up in flames and they lost everything but their lives. At this dead hour of the night, I can see those flames and eventually, I can see them in this house, growing bigger and taller like a plant in the earth. Night after night, I have mapped out how it would happen and what I could do when it does. It's as if it is inevitable. I know that this house will catch fire one day and I can't sleep because knowing that nobody will be awake when it happens makes my chest feel like it's about to burst open. My family don't realise the danger they could be in; they're all I have and I couldn't live if they didn't.

Once I couldn't stop thinking about the roof and how it was about to fall on top of me. Or if not that, then the floor underneath me was about to crumble and I would surely land atop my parents and brother beneath me, killing them. Then it would be my fault. On that particular occasion, I lay so still that my body ached. I was even afraid to cry too hard in case it shook the house at all. When I finally did fall asleep – after two trips downstairs – I was told that I had started talking in my sleep. My slumber was never peaceful and was always full of disturbances including talking, walking and sometimes screaming or shouting. The next thing I remembered after dozing off was my sister shaking me and telling me to shut up, that she couldn't sleep because I had been so noisy. As she stormed away again to her room, her feet pounded on the floors and I stopped breathing, knowing that now the house had no chance of standing for very long. I don't think I slept at all that night. I knew that if I fell asleep, I would never wake up again.

It's around this time of scanning through all the bad things in my head that I start to cry. So I get out of bed and hover at the top of the stairs for a while, listening carefully and hoping someone is still awake downstairs. Mum and Dad sleep down there and some nights I see the television light from their bedroom shining on the walls. That's very rare because everybody gets up really early in the mornings. It's pitch black at the bottom of the stairs and I feel guilty because I know I'll have woken Mum before I even knock on her door. She has gotten used to me doing this and listens for the creaks on the stairs that tell her I'm coming down to her. When I get to her room, I hold my breath so she can't hear me crying and say, 'I can't sleep.' I've been saying that every night for years.

In the darkness, a sigh flutters around the room which I know means Mum is trying to enjoy the next few moments in her warm bed before she has to step out into the cold. Dad is awake as well.

He's probably has a 12 hour shift starting at 8.00 am tomorrow, but won't give out to me because he knows I'm upset. I wait at the door, my toes icy on the wooden floors and my back sore and stiff as I try not move in the noisy hallway. For a moment, I wish I'd never come down. I tell myself that I could have just stayed upstairs and not been so selfish. However, I have sometimes gotten to my mother's door, turned around and gone back up to my room for this very reason. It never works out well and usually means I disturb my parents at a much later time and give myself more trips.

I can see movement in the darkness and Mum puts on her red dressing gown and walks me back to the landing. Though I feel better now because she's in the room with me, I can't shake my nerves fully because I know this is only temporary and that eventually, she will have to leave again. I can't let her do that. I beg and plead with her not to leave me alone, that I won't sleep and I'll be all alone.

'Leanne, what do you want me to do?' she says, wrapping me in her red dressing gown. It smells just like her and sometimes she'll let me have it for the night if I'm very upset. 'I can't stay up here all night.'

'Can I stay down with you and Dad?'

'Babe, I don't know. You need to stay in your own bed.'

'Please, Mum, please,' I whimper. She gives in and I go back to their room with her, wedging myself into the bed between my parents.

This starts to happen more and more and soon, my Dad has started sleeping in a different room. I don't even go upstairs anymore. Instead, I go straight to Mum's bed where the two of us argue until she finally just lets me stay with her. That moment when she says 'Alright then', is the happiest of my day. All my worries since waking have come down to just that and now, the worst has not happened for another night.

This place, this room is one of containment. I never want to leave it again. I want to board up the windows and the door and keep my mother here with me for ever. If I can do this, I will breathe easy again. I cling to this place for dear life because it's mine to keep. It will never cave in or catch fire while I'm in it. I will protect this place with my mother and it will protect me from the bullies at school and all the other bad things that happen outside of it. I don't want Mum to leave either in case something happens to her. I can't lose her so I don't let her go. I ask God to keep us here for ever.

WE'RE MUCH TOO EARLY in our story to start discussing the concept of control in detail. But for the moment, we can ascertain that I had issues with control since childhood. I never did develop much of a healthy sleeping pattern and still bounce from four to six hours of sleep a night, give or take. Of course, it doesn't matter much anymore and I've grown to relish those dark hours of solitude. During these sleepless childhood nights, however, my apparent inability to rest easy was horrific. It is something I often forget about and it's only now, as

I reflect on those lost snapshot flashes from my past that I recollect how horrible they were. No child should have anxieties so desperately violent that they cannot sleep for fear of losing control. But I think this was the case with me, even if I wasn't aware of it then. So knotted up about everything I could not control, my body seemed to switch a chord, following the trend and like everything else, I'd lost my authority over it even then. I swear, it often seems as if my bulimia was destined to happen, like she knew it long before I did. Looking back now I can see scattered traces of her among my dishevelled memories. It would be this lack of control that she would ultimately live off and seek to conquer.

The feeling was very familiar by the age of 18. Despite my already intoxicated state on the evening of Ami's birthday, my friends and I proceeded to the bar nonetheless for tequila shots, vodka and every other toxic-sounding spirit. Anxiety was starting to set in. I could feel that food from earlier turning over the workings of my body and making me sick. I thought if I drank more, the feelings would drown in the haze but it didn't work and I found my nerves slipping degenerately as the night progressed.

After my third round of shots – possibly more but I don't fully remember – we graduated to the dance floor. That's when the trouble started. The floor was packed full with people shuffling awkwardly. Sweat ran down my back and my mouth dried up with the intense heat. Pushing my head up for air from the sea of people, I was blinded by a bur of flashing lights overhead. Red, greens and yellows erupted in front of my eyes and I couldn't distinguish the faces of my friends anymore. The music pumped in the walls around us and I could feel a thunderous beat pulsing from my feet up to my hands. Pins and needles traced my fingertips and I was certain that my head would soon eject itself from my body and float to the roof. All the while, my stomach anchored me on the earth beneath my feet. The sting of toxins, the dead weight of food and the stain of cigarettes suddenly clamped down on me and I knew my body was about to forfeit the battle.

A wave of urgency flooded over me and I darted with such speed that I doubt my friends had even caught my rapid exit. With no care for who or what I bombed through in my path, the lavatory door finally shut behind me. I crashed to my knees and drew my head up over the toilet bowl, not looking down. It was vomiting and that was all. Not purging, vomiting. But the satisfaction and relief that ensued were feelings I would come to associate with that familiar position, hunched over the toilet bowl for a long time thereafter. I slumped back on my legs, exhausted and struggling a little for air.

'Leanne, you okay?' I heard Ami's voice come from behind the door.

'I'm fine, don't worry.' I called out to her. 'Go on back outside, I'll be out in a minute.'

Once I was sure she had left, my breathing steadied and my

body finally seemed to unite itself under just the one state of being. Aside from my knees feeling mildly weak, I was almost instantaneously relieved of the horrible sensations that had wrenched me moments before. I glanced back in the bowl, disgusted at the sight and waited for the adrenaline to leave my veins and bloodstream entirely. Sitting on that cubicle floor, my stomach now empty of the poisons that had previously inhabited it, it was as if my body was my own again. The emergency that reigned over me seemed to have dissolved so quickly since stepping into that cubicle and now here I was, feeling fine and completely in control of myself again. Yet when the time came for me to stand up and presume fixing my tousled make-up and clothes, I lingered on that floor. I still felt a little woozy from the drink and thought to myself that if vomiting had eased all that discomfort, perhaps just once more would make me feel completely sober.

It was debated for a few seconds in the back of my mind. I had already gotten sick, what difference would it make now? Leaning back over the toilet and nearly holding my breath due to the revolting stench, I strained my stomach and wretched at the air again and again. Nothing happened. So, committing to the thought of consequential relief, I dropped my bag to the floor and proceeded to slide my index finger down my throat. At first, my body was too tired for another round but with a little repetition and persuasion, the remainder of the contents in my stomach was emptied out in a matter of minutes. I was finished and now in a position to resume my night with ease.

Fixing my face in the mirror, it looked as if nothing had transpired. And I suppose, nothing had really; not beyond the usual evening a nightclub sees, whereby a teenager drinks too much and vomits in the nearest toilet. But what I remembered more than anything else that night was the vast difference of the feelings experienced before and after doing just that. My recklessness in the hours prior to dropping my head over that toilet left me strung out and wayward, while the feelings that seemed to render thereafter bounced between relief and a powerful sense of self-governance. Despite that, I'd be lying if I said that I didn't see that familiar monster flashing its devilish eyes at me from the reflection. Unable to behold the entirety of its ugliness, I hastened to rejoin my friends and continue in the birthday festivities.

Having reasonable command over ourselves is something most of us require, if not crave on a surface level. The methods we take in attaining that dominion status naturally vary from one individual to the next and the form in which said authority presents itself can be almost anything in the world. None of this occurred to me as I tidied myself in front of that mirror. But I knew that night that I had to regain control over myself. If I didn't, she would slip away and I may lose her forever. Continuously fasting was no way to live a life, certainly not for me and I always knew this to be true. Together, she and I had to find a way of maintaining our life together in such a way that it could last the test of time and still enable us to keep our devout secret. From that point on, our was to attain sustainability.

In hindsight, I think our endurance came in the form of bingeing itself. Binge eating was what commissioned our relationship. A key factor to the secrecy of how we lived, it ensured that we would never be accused of skipping meals. People, especially loved ones, can be extraordinarily easy to manipulate and I was getting better at it anyway. Eating in front of them and everyone else for that matter, had started to make me extremely uncomfortable; there was and remains nothing worse than someone actually witnessing me devour food, and as I imagine – or at least have convinced myself – that surely there is no worse a sight. Nevertheless, when I chose to binge, it would be timed around others. I concluded that if I were going to destroy my progress, I may as well feed into my own propaganda surrounding my eating habits at the same time. The precision with which she and I carried it out was usually impeccable.

To draw our attention back to the matter of what a binge really is, we must delve into the technicalities of the act itself. It's difficult to define where decision starts and disease finishes, as binges for me tended to transpire under a rather messy haze of confusion. Episodes like this could range from anything between 20 minutes to several hours and were fuelled by raw anxiety and panic. It wasn't just the hunger that sent me into this kind of feeding frenzy; cravings and the penetrating desire for the mere taste of food was enough in itself. Combined, the temptations of taste and the sharp wounds of hunger sent me spinning. I stopped living as a human then and reverted to some form of animal. The predator who dwelled within me burst out in great extravagance and gorged like nothing I had ever seen before. Nobody can eat like a bulimic can and I was like a wolf on the brink of perishing.

Speed was everything. I seemed to think that if I forced it all into my system fast enough, it wouldn't have time to morph its way into my bodily cells. The task was required to be skillfully crafted. While the rate at which I consumed this poison had to be of shocking dispatch, the contents had to be well ground-down; if not for the sake of an easier purge later, then even for my own peace of mind that masses of filth weren't infesting my body in huge chunks. Therefore, washing everything down with liquid between swallows was an irrevocable necessity. If for no other reason, it meant that there was a degree of lubrication both to my throat and the food itself when the time came for it to surrender its place in my body. Apparently I couldn't chew fast enough and I recall with great accuracy at a later stage in my illness, always contending with an aching jaw both during the binge and long after the purge.

When people think of bulimia, I assume they jump straight to the image of the purge itself, not realising that what leads to it is almost certainly just as grotesque a deed. For the purpose of our own understanding, perhaps we best draw on example in this case. Somewhere in that vast abyss of my disease, I have plucked a picture from my mind that has solidified itself in the deepest parts of my memory.

I was surely 19 on this particular occasion. Things were going well if I recall correctly and this, among other things, is usually detrimental to my fasting abilities. I have found that it's when I'm at my happiest that I am most likely to eat. When the world seems a complacent environment and I truly start to believe in the given false sense of security, I eat as 'normally' as I possibly can. I assume that this was one of those rare times. Or perhaps I was just famished past the point of planning ahead. Whatever the reason, it was 2.00 am when I sat up in front of the television, twitching with the hunger and dwelling on how the house had bedded down long ago and would certainly be asleep by now.

Don't ruin yourself, she hissed inside me, knowing my thoughts and desires. I knew she was right. Once momentarily unleashed, I knew I would let myself unravel completely. But I swear it had been like an abduction in which I was taken hostage by my body. I had no control from that point and sure enough, about an hour and a half after the thought first entered my brain, I sat exposed in front of an open fridge. By that stage, I had eaten three packets of crisps, a left-over steak dinner, two yoghurts, a bag of salted cashew nuts, a few chocolate bars and about a half litre of milk. It had only been 40 minutes. Still, I was not full. Too stuffed to so much as bend over for an extended amount of time, instead I plonked myself on the floor, rummaging around the cold shelves and feasting on a slice of lemon cheesecake in the process. With little to find, I settled on two bowls of chocolate cereal and one more packet of crisps.

My stomach had physically expanded like an inflated balloon and I was almost instantly light-headed from the rush of what I had done. I had eaten myself into a mental eclipse and would have cried, if my tear ducts had not been so incapacitated by the fat which smothered every inch of me. I felt like I had just poured liquid fat over myself like hot wax and was simply waiting for it to set. Collapsing back onto the couch, I was sweating profusely and thought my spine was about to snap as it attempted to uphold my weight.

The relief from my own starvation was temporary and short-lived. Those previous hunger pains had stopped long ago and so by the time I was through with my binge, I had already forgotten why I began it in the first place. Heavy shame set in. If anyone had seen me in those morning hours, they would probably never look at me the same way again, as I have never done so. The times spent bingeing, quite simply, remain some of the filthiest moments I have in recollection; they are the snapshots in time that are so violently maimed by my actions, I hate to think of them and indeed, my repulsive state within them. Bulimia nervosa is a disgusting illness in many ways for an alarming number of reasons, but this would be one of the most primitive of those reasons. Looking back even still, all I see is a mildly obese teen; breathless and panting, sweat rolling down her back, bits of every kind of food wedging itself between her teeth, tongue flailing, jaw throbbing, stuffing garbage down her throat and nearly taking her fingertips off in the process.

The humiliation attached to this picture is festered deep inside and even now, I am ashamed of it. I'm ashamed of who I was and what I did. But nothing I have felt since comes close to the swelling degradation in which I drowned then. That voice in my head stopped screaming and the silence was penetrating and life-altering. I had disgraced both of us to a point whereby I don't think she even knew what to say. In the wake of her apparent absence – life, disease, purpose – everything stopped. The haunting nothingness of her eerie silence broke my heart. I thought the world had stopped turning and that time stood still. I was all alone then and more than ever before, that was when I truly hated myself.

I would rather die, I thought to myself. If this was who I really was, I would rather die than live as this. She would never forgive me, living as the monster I knew myself to be. Surely even God could not forgive me. And I was certain I would never forgive myself. I thought about waking the next morning and how the damage I had done tonight would be seen like scales on my skin. That notion, and the now encroaching feeling that life without her had no purpose, made me want to pull the plug on my own existence. Yes, I would have rather died. I dwelled so long upon the thought, that I sometimes wonder why or how I'm even still here today. It became more and more likely every time I felt that shame hang on me like a damp cloth. The potential reality of my own suicide is still something I often hate myself for whenever I think of how close I came to it.

I suppose this is why I saw purging as such a positive facet to my life. If I hadn't purged, God knows what actions I would have taken instead. It is for this reason that I believed purging, and bulimia herself, to be somewhat of a saviour to me. If she had not provided me with the mental tools to do the things I did, I shudder to think what I would have done instead. But alas, we're racing ahead and should restrain ourselves for the time being from launching into the purging process.

After the night of Ami's 19th birthday, something had to be done. I had seen the monster again and was terrified to think what would happen if I let it out. I had been out of control for too long, had packed on all those lost pounds and had watched as my life started to unfold all over again. There exists a very fine line between dieting and eating disorders, and after years of teetering around that border, I had finally crossed it months ago. I think I knew this somewhere inside of me and where I usually typed 'diet' into the internet search engine, I know typed the words 'anorexia', 'bulimia' and 'emaciated' again and again. The words, as well as the facts and images that followed them, became an obsession. This was my pastime and soon I would make sure it was my entire life too.

The abundance of pro-ED sites on the internet would probably shock people who have never lived this way. For those who are unfamiliar with these websites, a pro-ED website is a place where eating disorders are endorsed, glorified and warmly condoned. They go so far as to affectionately name the most popular and well known diseases such as Ana (anorexia), Mia (bulimia) and ED (eating disorders in general). I feel obligated to verbally bash and condemn such places but even from my post-recovery point of view, I still can't bring myself to do so. Though we could never undermine the dangers of these online communities and the toxic environments they breed, there simply isn't any malice in their creation. What we are discussing here is sick people talking to other sick people, seeking refuge and understanding. To judge would only prove to accelerate our own ignorance. Moreover, I simply can't lie to you dear reader and therefore must admit that in these underground worlds, I felt I was finally home. The sentiment I once had for these hidden places and silenced people is, to this day, tender to the touch.

It was more than a hot-spot for 'thinspo'; this haven and these people provided the company I had beseeched for so long. Their words, struggles and even personalities leapt from the screen and straight into the most empathetic part of me. I knew these people as I know myself because we shared our darkest demons in that place. Free of persecution and the constant feeling of abnormality, in that safe space, I could step out from the shadows even if only briefly. I was myself for the first time in a long time. I was the self that she, my Mia, had created and I wasn't embarrassed about who I was or what she had made of me. If anything, I heard the affecting stories of others and even begged of her to take me in as she had done so with these people. This was her mercy and she was my own personal heroine. Mia, Ana, ED – whoever she was, I now wanted to be hers entirely.

No friend and no boyfriend could ever have what I gave to her because as I wasn't worthy of them, so they were not worthy of her. Unable to take back all the self-worth I had given away of myself before, instead it had been merely shifted from one place to another. That worth fell into her hands; the hands with which she caressed me from time to time if I was good.

There in that terrain, the one which rests behind closed doors, tucked under baggy clothes and sizzling beneath burnt-out eyes, I had found my soul mates. They knew what it was to hate yourself. They understood how important it was to step on a scale every 45 minutes. They underwent the burden of sacrificing old friends and former loved ones for her benevolence. They felt the loneliness that plagued you during late hours awake in bed and the stabbing knife of hunger during daylight. Whomever the girl, she was the me of Jacksonville and Seattle; the me of Brisbane and Sydney; the me of Sheffield and Manchester; whoever she was, we were the same person because despite the different lives we lead, we stood united in our underworld of misery and depravity. Suddenly, I wasn't so alone.

Aside from the camaraderie between the people who frequented such sites, I found a degree of freedom in having such a place in which to retire. I traipsed endlessly from page to page, soaking it up and breathing it in. I accepted the normality in which this world was being executed. It was as if this lifestyle and this state of being were so obviously natural to us all. I teetered my way through tips and advice, ways in which to properly conduct the progression of my disease. I discovered how best to suppress the hunger that was now a permanent part of me and more importantly, how to conceal everything with an almost professional air of efficiency. Moved and softened, I read the painful accounts of others and watched as they poured themselves into their words, seeking reconciliation and acceptance. The empathy and longing for their well-being remains as strong today as it was then.

Fasting competitions and gospels about the glory of eating disorders left little doubt that I was living as I was intended to. This, surely, was my destiny in life and the path God had set out for me. He had meant for me to share my life with my bulimia, I was convinced of it. There was a false sense of completion to who I was and my place in the world. I belonged here and thus, belonging anywhere else didn't matter to me all that much anymore. Furthermore, these websites helped me justify my new lifestyle.

This isn't a problem, I started hearing her whisper. *This is a blessing in disguise and our gift to the world. Together, we are worth the air we breathe. United we stand and alone, neither of us may even dream to exist.* I had discovered the Holy Grail and it was there, amidst those black feelings and lost memories. I was home.

My obsession, which had been born in the tiniest embryo of my mind, turned outwards and visuals worked in sync with feeling. What

I saw corresponded greatly to what I felt thereafter. The problem was that even my ability to interpret such imagery was, in itself, contorted and insufficient for lack of a better word. Online 'thinspo' of celebrities and model-like figures wasn't enough anymore because it could not attack my senses in the way reality did. Only through reality could my sharp thoughts and swelling feelings take life and walk the streets in front of me. Through the reality of my disease, those thoughts and emotions soon appeared everywhere. They were the kick in my morning coffee, the smoke from my cigarettes and every interaction I had with people. The epidemic had spread at a feverous speed and no longer existed only in my mind; finally, the world seemed to live in its reflection.

The pro-ED websites did not create my bulimia, but they crafted her. She was shaped through their existence, among many other things, as we continue to explore. Reality was found when I saw women exposing themselves on those sites. They weren't models, or actors or a-list faces who walked red carpets for a living. They were genuine people living secret lives and were everything I could ever dream to be. I started to believe that there was an authenticity to their eating disorders and not to my own. What determined this credibility and degree of success in my bulimia would take various shapes and forms, which we will discuss at a later point.

But for the time being, I think I can safely make the note that it was these websites that classified my own eating disorder as bulimia nervosa. I say this because I learned – similarly to how a student in a classroom learns – the differences between what it meant to be Ana and what it meant to be Mia. Equally, I sought to define myself within the given conditions of the disorders I was learning about. I think once the disease was comfortably instilled in the workings of my mind, choices like these were easy because I wasn't the person making them anymore. So, perhaps I didn't choose to have an eating disorder. It chose me. Yet, once in full swing, I suppose I chose to classify my eating disorder to bulimia; I felt empowered by the very decision itself.

I knew I could never live the life of an anorexic. Though I had developed an adversity to food and a general discomfort with eating, I still never envisioned myself sacrificing it completely. Bulimia seemed an obvious answer to all my problems. It would be mine to keep forever and sometimes I wonder if it was as simple as "picking" it. I mean, nobody forced me to put my finger down my throat the first time I purged. I think sometimes though that by that stage I just chose to accept the lifestyle which already existed in my mind. It wasn't a process of "picking"; it was one of submission.

Ultimately, what seems to define bulimia in the minds of others is the purge. The reality is that purging does not occur without a binge and sometimes a fast before it. My bulimia was defined by all three and as a result, was well underway in its manifestations long before I ever regurgitated my first meal.

But that crucial point was always going to come. It arrived sooner than I could have ever anticipated. That's the thing with an eating disorder; for something that takes years to develop, when it finally shows itself, it snowballs. I was riding a free-fall and for some of the time, I rather enjoyed it. Granted, it went on to become the most dangerous and devastating chapter in my young life. But it wasn't all bad, not at the beginning anyway. One doesn't persist in this kind of existence unless one truly feels that something is to be gained from it. God help me, I really believed in it.

The various facets of my illness aside, I look back on the decisions I made during that time in my life with utter embarrassment. I've had so many moments of wishing I could return to that place, go back to that girl and shake her. I would tell her that it's never going to be worth it; that if she continues this way, she will damage her family, her friendships, her education and future. But most importantly, I would tell her that she will damage her mental health almost beyond repair. Perhaps it's a good thing I can't do that because if I did, who knows what kind of person would be writing this, or if indeed such an account would even exist.

Both the fast and the binge have, until this point, been the blurriest stages in my disorder. Denial reigned through them and thus, distorted my recollection a great deal. It would be a very long time before I would ever admit openly what I had finally admitted to myself, as my denial to others outlasted my self denial by a large stretch. But in my own mind, there was no doubt anymore about what I had become. I knew it before I had even purged. Finally answering the screams of that person who lived in my mind, I thought to myself, *Yes. I am bulimic.*

THE PURGE

I STARED AT THE toilet bowl in front of me, now painted in an array of oranges and skin coloured pinks. I was light-headed and my vision had blurred slightly, but still I could make out small chunks of food that swished around the basin. Watery noodles were still sliding their way downwards, while my mother's chocolate cake had sunk under the water surface at the bottom. That had been rather painful to regurgitate. The spongy texture of it kept getting caught in my throat and landed with a *plonk* when it hit the base of the toilet. But by now, I was a pro at this. Knowing that I had limited time before someone knocked on the bathroom door, I put my index finger in my mouth, wet it with saliva and slid it back down my throat.

Purging had become the most important part of my day. Depending on circumstance and opportunity, sometimes I could only purge once or twice a day. This meant that when the time came to expel the food that riddled my weak body, I would commit to the moment entirely. I knew that it would be hours before I could do it again. I suppose this is why I never stopped fasting completely. I usually only ate when I was sure I could purge afterwards. In the beginning, breaking my fasts was an almost involuntary act. Overpowered by the hunger sirens that sent electric shocks up and down my body, I would binge purely out of desperation. After the first bite – no matter how small it may have been – I told myself that I'd ruined everything already and thus gorge until I thought I would burst.

Now, however, I was more strategic and meticulous about my eating. I had the tune down to a note and played it with flawless execution. An ideal day would see me fasting until dinner time, when it was nearly impossible to get out of eating the family meal. I would eat as was expected, all the while washing it down with buckets of water. After dinner, I would take my daily shower. While most people showered in the mornings, my parents had simply accepted that I just preferred to wash up after tea time. It suited everyone because nobody took as long in a shower as I did; sometimes I'd be in there for almost 40 minutes. But it was routine now and little to no questions were ever asked. Even 40 minutes never seemed like enough time. I would purge for anywhere between 15 to 30 minutes, saving time at the end to give myself a quick wash over.

Such a day was a rarity though; I grew up in a house that was always busy with people coming and going. The key was balance and timing. Most of my days at that time were spent as a trapeze artist on a tightrope, never putting a foot out of place and always fastidiously coordinated. I hated eating in front of people but for the sake of proving a point, I usually began a binge not long before my family left the house for their various errands, jobs and social coffees. Once alone, the binge would kick into full swing and I would blitz the entire ordeal to the point of a ravenous blackout, leaving myself just enough time to vomit before they came home. In this way, I was reassured that they would see the used pots and pans, the chocolate wrappers, the milky cereal bowls and whatever else I had used to feed myself. I wouldn't have to eat again until dinner, which could be remedied during my usual shower or bath.

The purge was not always intended. I remember once or twice starting a binge with a fruit salad, convinced that I would merely eat healthily for the day. But once in the momentum of my feeding frenzy, I usually consoled myself with the knowledge that the food would not stay in my stomach. I couldn't just leave it there. And, on occasion, I started regurgitating before I'd even finished my binge. For the most part, however – and certainly quite late into my bulimia – the act of purging was premeditated, enabling me to plan for it in advance.

I avoided meat while bingeing because I knew it would be very painful to vomit back up. Similarly, pizzas and chips were always a struggle for me. That's not to say I didn't binge on them though; I ate whatever my fingers touched but consciously aimed to eat more water-based foods that wouldn't hurt me while purging. Noodles and eggs seemed to just slip right out with the correct push and they always featured in my binge if the purge was calculated. If this wasn't the case, I would have to just accept what needed to come up and get on with it.

Snapping back to the task at hand, I hadn't finished my purge yet. I checked the time on my phone and saw that I only had about ten minutes left until I would have to wash up and return to the world outside the bathroom door.

Hurry up you fat cow!, she roared in my head. If I didn't do it now, I knew I would have to listen to that unforgiving voice for the rest of the night. The soft whispers that she graced me with before had long since disappeared and were replaced with screams of abuse and filthy words. She had poisoned my thoughts with words and phrases I never envisioned myself ever thinking, let alone using in reference to myself. Finger down my throat and the blood rushing to my face; this was her moment of glory and when she was most alive in my life.

I'd gotten most of it up by now but had to continue until I was sure I'd left nothing in my stomach. The noise of the shower was thunderous and blasted overhead, while the scalding water steamed up the tiny room. I was sweating from my head to my toes and could feel droplets of perspiration running through my hair and down my neck. Even without the hot shower turning the bathroom into a 40 minute sauna, I probably would have been sweating anyway. After a few minutes of purging, my adrenaline would pump up a gear and make the blood that ran in my veins sizzle.

I no longer knew what was running down my face. It was a mixture of sweat from my brow, mucus running from my nose and flooding tears from my eyes as I gagged. Taking a breather for a few seconds, I would look at myself in the mirror, dazed and breathless.

Vomit and spit traced the corners of my mouth, while my cheeks puffed out red and swollen. Everything about my face seemed to puff like that when I purged. My eyes bulged and I swore on several occasions that I could see a vein about to burst open on my forehead. Splashing my face with cold water, I couldn't lose momentum or else I would be too exhausted to finish. I knelt back over, my knees buckling beneath me and a fresh piece of tissue in my left hand. I caressed my index finger in my mouth for a while, warming it and sufficiently lubricating it. Ready for the next round, I shoved it down my throat.

I wonder sometimes if my gag reflex had become in some way desensitised. More and more, my finger down my throat would have little effect on me and I was forced to wiggle it around and violently reef it from side to side. Only then would I gag, usually holding my breath at the same time. I would retch several times before giving my stomach that extra push to expel the food. With each episode of regurgitation, I arched my neck and my jaw would lock open. If I'd consumed all the right kinds of food, it would spew out effortlessly and in huge amounts. In other cases – like that of the aforementioned chocolate cake – it would hit the toilet bowl in large chunks, clogging my throat along the way and leaving me gasping for air.

Every time I choked, my throat would sting. In the frenzy of trying to retch, I had scraped the back of my throat with my fingernail. Every time I vomited, it prickled as if a needle was being jabbed into it. I had to be quick about removing my finger again; several times when I wasn't, vomit, bile and pieces of food would eject out onto my hand and cover my fingers. The smell that lined them would give me a headache and I'd have to wash my hands, costing me more of my precious time in the bathroom.

I was certain I could have done it even without the shower running in the background but never wanted to take that chance. If the secrecy I enjoyed in that room was ever compromised, I knew my relationship with her would change forever. Still, I endeavoured to be as quiet as possible and by this stage, had mastered it. Despite the ease of vomiting up liquid-based foods, there was little I could do to prevent the sharp clap one could hear when they splashed into the toilet. I knelt to the side of the bowl and aimed for its inner wall, hoping the noise would be lessened. Four or five retches later and a flood of orange liquid and chunks splashed against the basin at such velocity that I was thankful for the noisy shower. The later into the purge I got, my stomach heaved and made a most distinct noise along with it. I once compared the sound to that of an animal squeezing out its last breaths. By the end of my self-induced vomiting, when finally nothing was left to come out, the sound was usually very loud and, to a large extent, mentally satisfying. Job done; the sound of emptiness had confirmed it.

Nevertheless, I was very quiet. I couldn't control what happened once the food had come up but demanding a solid command over myself was a necessity in these endeavours and I did so perfectly, most of the time. Every time I retched and heaved another spell from the pit of my stomach and up to my throat, with it I suppressed every noise by holding my breath and tensing every muscle that ran from my abdomen to my face. With every gag and each spew of vomit, my body lifted a heavy weight of skilled silence. I read on one of my beloved pro-ED websites, that sometimes it was effective to simply never remove your finger from your throat and thus allow for an uninterrupted continuation of purging. I could never do this. If I did, I would almost certainly pass out from a lack of oxygen.

As it was, breathing was a strain and most of the time, I thought I would collapse anyway. All the blood that pumped through my veins hurtled its way to my face until I felt like the skin encasing it would burst. My legs often fell slightly numb and in those moments when I was unsure that they still stood below me, I just knew it would not be too long before they cracked and left me crashing to the bathroom tiles.

So often, I considered even giving in and just relinquishing my efforts in trying to satisfy that harrowing voice in my mind. My stomach was being shredded in two directions and left at an abrupt and painfully misguided standstill. A vile image to imagine, I have no doubt, but the truth is that sometimes I fought my body's natural urges for fear of it disrupting my very important purge. I hated having to leave a meal too long in my body because it meant that eventually, my system would attempt to digest it and ultimately, of course, rid itself of it at some stage. I couldn't let this happen before I'd purged. If I did, it meant that every fatty component of that meal would be fully absorbed and broken down before finally leaving; the damage would have already been done.

Instead, I was faced with an urgency like no other, whereby I had to purge before I ever needed to use the toilet. If I thought I was in need of it, I would vomit until the very sensation had finally disappeared. As if doing so would somehow shove a hand down to my stomach, into my digestive system and reef it all out before it had time to complete its task of poisoning my body. Even if I couldn't get it all, by God, I would get most.

I measured the short-lived progress in a number of ways. All of which required my eyes open and alert to what was happening before me. Colouration was always the most obvious form of mental documentation; chocolate, brown; yoghurt, pink; carbohydrates, usually yellow. It was simple. Depending on what I'd eaten, I knew what had been cleared from my body. Rarely were the colours so vibrant as they had been on entering my mouth, but nonetheless I became accustomed to what certain foods looked like upon regurgitation and thus, was always aware of what was left to be purged. This knowledge was developed only over time and as a result of many purges because food – subject to how long it has been in your stomach – can look different when it makes its return in the opposite direction.

It also influenced my binge to a great extent because it meant having to take mental snapshots of what I was eating. In such a short space of time, as well such an inflamed process of thinking, taking note of what I was consuming was sometimes impossible. It was almost like an out-of-body experience and meant that disciplining myself to plan ahead for my purge was a conscious effort.

Taste was another form of accurate chronicling. This was dependent on how soon after a binge I could proceed with the purge. But if straight away – or even very soon after – the food I'd ingested would still resemble the taste with which it infiltrated my body. Therefore, distinguishing between the entire pizza I'd eaten, the bowl of pasta, the multiple chocolate bars and the four or more slices of crumble became all too easy. The real trick was making sure I had gotten all liquids up. Having a terrible weakness for milk, I often chose to wash it all down with a cold pint glass of the stuff rather than water. I hoped that it would somehow cling to the various foods in my inflated stomach and make an appearance along with their debut. If the chocolate wasn't quite so brown or tasted a little watery while vomiting, I was sure that it had absorbed all the milk thus easing its somewhat violent exit.

Usually, my mouth would dry out as I spat into the toilet bowl. After each splatter of food into the basin, a trail of spit would surely follow, dangling from my lips, refusing to disconnect itself from my exhausted mouth. This is why I kept a bundle of tissue paper gripped in my left hand; if not to simply dry my lips off, then to break the wet string that stuck to them. The tissue was eventually drowned in no time and feeling disgusted with myself enough, I hated holding a used one and discarded it mid-way through my session. With my nose stinging from the mucus circling around it, my face heating up and my heartbeat pulsing in each temple, all sensations would at some point direct themselves back to my chest. It was as if I could fully feel the strain being put on my heart. From there, it bled out onto the bones that encased it. They ached like someone had taken a bat to them.

I'm bruising *my bones*, I thought. If my chest bones weren't about to rupture, at the very least the spindly bone and cartilage of my neck was about to snap and crack out, splitting my skin along the way. I've had images of myself walking out of the bathroom with a bone protruding somewhere between my jaw and collar bone.

Knowing when to stop was obvious by every measure. For one thing, my attempted silence could no longer prevail. Struggling to lift anything from my now empty stomach, a ball in the base of my throat would gag involuntarily and produce a sound similar to a cough but a little more sudden. Moreover, the substance released from my mouth no longer resembled anything of food in smell, taste or texture. It was yellow and off-coloured orange bile from the pit of my gut that tasted like poison and stung my nostrils when the smell filtered upwards. I once mentally compared it to urine, as if I was now vomiting my own urine. It was time to stop.

I usually hovered over the toilet a little longer after finishing my purge, afraid of standing upright too quickly and falling backwards from the rush. My weak hand still clutching a drowned ball of tissue, dabbed around my mouth. Head spinning and my shoulders shaking, I would lean over the sink and attempt to regain some of the lost consciousness.

Silence.

She was gone and in her place a cut-throat hush that lingered in the air. She had disappeared for now and I was the only thing that was left behind. In those moments, an iron curtain descended. There was no sky above me nor ground below me. For all I knew, all oxygen had been sucked from the planet into a vacuum elsewhere. Despite all the trust I'd placed in her, she never failed in the extent of her cruelty after purging. In the aftermath of my self-induced oblivion, I was truly alone and I hated it. She was not there to seduce me with words or intoxicate me with her thoughts. She left me alone in that hole and in that darkness to suffer. I knew this moment would come and yet had done what I was told anyway because I wanted to believe she would still be there afterwards. Instead, the naively anticipated hope of her reassurance was replaced with wounding guilt. I could not hide from the feeling because she burnt the bridges of comfort I walked upon. I had done this to myself. In those moments I knew she had never really been there and only I had caused this grotesque scene. It was my guilt to bear; not hers or anyone else's. I owned that guilt like a crucifix strapped to my shoulders.

Slumping my way into the running shower, I turned the heat down. Propelled from the adrenaline, my skin usually scorched at an alarming temperature and I welcomed the cold water on my back. I was still weak and unable to stand. Consequently, I squatted down into the bathtub, icy water running from my head and down my spine. Too ashamed to so much as lift my head towards a world I was not worthy of, I pulled my knees up to my chest, held them tight and buried my face downwards. My head was too sore to cry but I could never hold back the tears. I wept helplessly beneath the heavy droplets from above. My back hurt the most now. It was like someone had wrapped the mouth of a wrench around my deteriorating spine; if I moved too suddenly, that mouth would shut instantly and surely fracture my bone like a twig.

I moved slowly, still shaking. When the time came to abandon my spot beneath the icy shower, I resumed my position above the toilet, beholding the masterpiece in all its horror. Before me I saw everything I hated about myself. All my darkness sat in front of me; my body and mind now cleansed of it. I had exorcised all the demons that corrupted my mind. And in the ever encroaching silence, hell no longer existed only in my head. It now surrounded me, staring me in the eye from the well of a toilet. But with one flush, I composed myself, knowing that the world outside the door was waiting for me again. Show time was drawing near once more.

Easy, she soothed, finally returning to her place in some mental crevice. *Don't let them know. It's our little secret.*

142

There was no escape. I knew that the door between this place and that of the world beyond it would, in some way, be shut forever. Freedom was a lost dream and escape seemed to have never even existed.

I AM TEN YEARS old. I don't like doing knick-knacks because I know it's bold and see how angry Mum and Dad get when it's done to them. We will all be sitting together watching television, when the doorbell rings. Dad will answer it but the children who rang the bell have run off. When Dad comes back into the sitting room, he's really angry and curses about the bold kids who did it.

I don't want to be one of those naughty children, but here I am, playing knick-knacks on my neighbours. If Mum knew she would be so angry with me. We have targeted my next-door neighbour's house and after three knick-knacks, the man who lives next door is fuming. We can hear him shouting in his sitting room about the children who keep doing it. While the girls laugh hysterically, all I can think about is how my Dad does the same thing when it happens to us. I wonder if my Dad or my neighbour, Mick, ever feel embarrassment that they are being picked on. When I think about this, suddenly I feel sick and guilty. I want to stop playing the game; not because I could get into trouble but because I feel as horrible as the children who do this to my Dad and wonder if it would upset him knowing that his daughter is just as bold.

The only reason we've played a knick-knack on Mick's house

so much is because we won't get caught. When someone rings the doorbell, we all run to the lane at the side of my house. Though I'm too short, the girls are tall enough to reach over the gate and unhook the latch, releasing us into the back garden and keeping us safe when Mick comes into his driveway, his face red with anger and his hands on his hips. We hide behind the big gate, watching him through the cracks. The girls are battling with their silent chuckling and I'm simply trying to steady my breathing, while my heart races with fear and remorse.

'It's great we can get in here' one of the girls says, fighting back the laughter. 'We can do this all day!'

But I don't want to do this all day. Aside from the growing twitch of guilt festering in my tummy, it's nearly teatime and Mum will come outside to call me very shortly. But I can't tell the girls I want to stop because then they'll tell me I'm a goody two-shoes and won't play with me again. Instead, I say I can only do one more knick-knack because I have to go inside for dinner soon. This seems to satisfy them. Because it's the last one, the girls tell me that they want to watch from across the road.

'I'll go unlatch the gate now for you,' one of them says walking back down the lane.

'And then we'll run over and hide behind the bushes,' says the other. 'We'll wave at you so you know when to ring the bell.' I don't want to do this. Even though I've been playing the game, I've never rung the doorbell myself and just know I'm going to do something to ruin everything. But before I know it, the girls are running across the road and positioning themselves behind the hedges to watch. I'm standing alone waiting for their signal when panic sets in. I tell myself that I should have gone into my house ages ago. I should be sitting with my parents now, waiting for my dinner and out of trouble's way. I consider just running inside now and not saying goodbye to the girls. In fact, my feet start to move in the direction of my front door when at long last, I see a white hand waving frantically from the bushes.

Frozen to the ground on which I stand, I'm trapped and now cannot get out of what I'm about to do. Not wanting to prolong the agony of my own guilt, I make up mind and run to Mick's porch. In my head, I whisper to myself, 'Just do it. Get it over with and go home.' My finger presses the button before I even tell it to do so and not waiting to hold the buzzing sound for every long, I dart away, nearly taking the doormat with me. I reach the big gate down the lane and am so relieved to know that escape waits just beyond it. I push forward against the brown wood, only to realise that the door isn't swinging open.

'No, no, no, no!' I start to shake it violently. I can hear the latch clicking every time I try to push it open. The girls never opened the latch. Now here I am, trapped on the wrong side of it.

The world feels like it's closing in on me, as I desperately try to reach above the gate. I can feel the latch but I'm too short to fully unhook it. I jump up and down, trying to get a hold over it but it comes to nothing; that door is shut and I can't get it open no matter how hard I try. All I can think is how much I wish I could get it open. Beyond it waits escape and safety. As it stands, I'm being held hostage by my own body on this side of it. If only I was taller and I could reach it.

'You little...' I hear behind me. Mick has discovered me trying to hide in the lane, still cowering at the closed gate. I'm backed into a corner now. Knowing that Mum will find out in a matter of moments and that the girls have probably disappeared, I press my hand to the wooden door and feel defeat beneath my hand. My mother sent me to bed without supper that night and rightly so; the poor woman had to endure a long and angry tangent from her neighbour. She suspected the girls' involvement in the mischief but as I expected even then, they had been quick to disappear when trouble struck. I never sought to implicate them in the consequences and bit my tongue on the matter.

With my purge finally finished and my mind was calm once more, I stood in the bathroom, still exhausted and with my hand placed upon the wooden door, caressing it similarly to how I had done all those years ago. The barriers we face in life are so often the ones we create in our minds. As a child I couldn't open that wooden gate because my body prevented me from doing so. As a teenager, it seemed I couldn't open that door because my mind now held me hostage. The world that waited beyond it now was no longer one of safety or escape. Instead, I knew every time that I opened that door, it would be to a life of psychological insecurity and emotional entrapment. She – that cerebral leech who clung to all my thoughts – convinced me of this fact. Only with her could I find and maintain an asylum of mental armour.

I was still that frightened ten-year-old, snared on the wrong side of the gate. Still in that world of guilt and disgrace, I hovered at the door for a few moments after every purge. I would never be able to reach that latch at the back of my mind and I would never leave this place alive. This, I was sure of at least.

My post-purge experiences had the ability to vary greatly from day to day. Sometimes, I would be so revved up with adrenaline that my energy would manage to persist through the ordeal itself and long thereafter if required. For the most part, however, I underwent a form of lethargic paralysis. After slipping into some comfortable and, of course, baggy clothes, all I could bring myself to do was light up a smoke at the kitchen table. There was nothing like puffing on a cigarette after a purge. Together, she and I had been the puppeteers of our body, pushing it to all extremities and limits, only to finish with a divine sense of accomplishment. We had truly earned the fag to take the edge off.

Watching the smoke dance in front of my face, I recalled some of the first times I ever put a cigarette to my lips. After a mere two years of smoking, already the nicotine rushes had disappeared. Wasn't that why I started; because the nicotine rushes were so good? I couldn't remember. Probably not, anyway; I've no doubt I began smoking simply to fulfil my own ideal of what made me acceptable to my peers. Either that, or it had been a good substitute for weed, which I smoked for a time but simply couldn't afford to continue with.

Whatever the reason, I very rarely got any kind of kick from cigarettes anymore. My smoking habit reminds me greatly of my purging. In the beginning, both had offered some degree of relief and satisfaction. But as time travelled on, each became something I was plagued with rather than something I chose to do. They were both addictions in their own right and even long after the action stopped providing the desired effect, I continued to smoke and purge relentlessly.

Initially, self-induced vomiting provided the escape I needed from everyday stresses. It was proof that I could use my body to satisfy the wailing hunger that penetrated my thoughts. Yet the feeling wasn't sustainable. The first time I purged wasn't long after Ami's 19th birthday and at the time, it had provided me with a sense of exaltation; it was liberation from the food I had become so deathly afraid of. But purging soon became a daily occurrence and my memories of the collective hours spent vomiting up meals and sleeping thereafter have manifested exclusively into the aforementioned description.

Thus, sometimes it's difficult to remember why I did it in the first place, much the same I struggle to remember why I picked up my first cigarette.

Losing weight in general had the same effect, as I recall. We all know that feeling of stepping onto the scales after a difficult diet. You've been working very hard and hesitantly put your first foot atop the board. Still a little scared that for some unknown reason you'll have shed no pounds at all, you hold your breath slightly, waiting for the verdict to tally down below. For me, the first time I saw the tremendous drop in numbers on the scales, I rode on a cloud of ecstasy. It was never going to last though, that feeling of unrestricted happiness. Moreover, no matter what I did, I simply couldn't keep my weight down. It fluctuated for months from one extremity to the next, which I think is what scared loved ones the most. I wonder sometimes if what terrified them was how apparently 'skinny' I had become or simply the rate at which I could both drop and gain weight. Either way, I never wanted to let that momentary feeling of happiness go.

At first, I think I believed that if I could simply avoid gaining weight that it would be enough to sustain my elation. It was, for a while. Soon, though, I stopped being complimented on how wonderful I looked and the novelty of fitting into a size ten faded away. I just wanted to get that feeling back. In this way, I suppose it really was such an innocent pursuit on one level.

'I just want to be happy.' I uttered the words to myself time and time again. Such a harmless hope; I never knew what it could turn into. Happiness was a mere superficiality by that stage though and indeed, it isn't impossible that in fact I didn't really want it either. It was as if by keeping me miserable, she could control everything I did in my pursuit of this allusive and now entirely alien concept. Furthermore, I came to understand the notion of "self-harm" under a much broader dictation. Now cast under the heading of an "eating disorder victim", in recent years I've had to simply widen my once narrow-minded scope on the complexity of human beings, both as a collective society as well as the individuals that compose it. Self-harm has been one of these complexities.

Much like an eating disorder or any other form of mental illness, I make the assumption that self-harming is an issue widely misunderstood and even still, I make no claim to knowing much about it. But the term did enter my head several times in one form or another during this period of my life. This is largely due to the fact that I saw my purging so often as a form of necessary punishment for the crime of my own worthlessness. Never before had I understood how or why any individual could take a blade to their own skin and indulge in tearing open the flesh.

At that point, however, I think I at least *began* to, even if only a little. You see, for every measure I lost in my own worth and purpose for even being on this planet, my reasons for purging gained profoundly. Very often, it was a form of retribution or even compensation for various facets of my life that simply could not be disciplined under my grip. A failed test, an argument in the home, a moment of mild social embarrassment; whatever the given occasion, I would convince myself of my own fault on the matter and thus, simply accept the fact that I needed to be punished and I needed to suffer.

When the body suffers, the mind flourishes, she told me. And I clung to that creed for the longest time. The more pain I could endure, the stronger I became and surely the less guilt ridden I would feel in time. Like a blade ripping open the flesh, my purging ripped me open from the inside out. If I had the capacity to withstand instantaneous physical pain, I think I would have even considered taking a razor to my leg. Because after so long of living in that hole, I would have rather felt pain than nothing at all; I just wanted to feel something again. You reach a milestone in such illnesses when denial lifts and you realise that the things you do are truly damaging both to yourself and to others. By then, however, you learn to not care and you embrace the notion that this method of self-harming is both deserved and satisfying.

Equally, I began to use my cycles of fasting, bingeing and purging against those around me. So often it presented itself as a form of protest. If ever disgruntled or deeply upset by the actions or words of others, channelling that anxiety into those private hours spent on the bathroom floor became mentally healing for me. It was a silent protest, unknown to everyone but myself. Nevertheless, it was powerful and moving, as if the vibrations of its cause, whatever the case could be felt all over the world.

Despite my warped dedication to my illness, I did have days

when I questioned what I was doing to myself. I doubt anyone who ever suffered from an eating disorder could claim that they never lingered over the thought that they should stop. Once or twice, I even went as far as to try and eat both healthily and regularly. The goal of losing weight never came into question, merely the methods to do so. But on these occasions, no matter how little or indeed healthy the choice of food, it felt too unnatural to carry on. One morning on campus, when I was about ten minutes too early for a lecture, I thought to buy myself a granola bar and bottle of water. Food can be incredibly distracting when the body has become so used to being entirely void of it. Once consumed, all attention and focus drives itself to this unthinkable act. My mind and sometimes my body reacted to food in the same way that white blood cells react to a foreign invader. My whole system seemed to have turned against it, or at least I convinced myself of this. As my mind did overtime in mapping what was happening to the food inside me, it tricked my stomach into a false sense of pain. I would become entirely convinced of sudden abdominal cramps. Apparently, they were intolerable.

Sitting in that lecture, I could feel the granola bar contaminating my body. I tried to ignore the growing anxiety but my nerves, as usual, started in their pursuit of cutting off my airways again. I stopped writing and had switched off from what was being said long ago. I just couldn't focus. Rushing out of the lecture theatre rather abruptly and not caring if anyone noticed, I scurried for the nearest bathroom. It was empty, thank God.

'It was just one bar, that's all,' I soothed myself. It didn't take long to get it up and alas, I was greeted with the familiar bite of devout emptiness. Purging was more than just a means of expelling food and more than just a form of self-harm; in the twisted logic that ticked around the back of my head, it was cleansing for my mind and body. While food made me feel dirty, tainted and unworthy, purging made me feel clean again. A psychological rebirth took place with every episode of self-induced vomiting.

All this isn't to say that purging is exclusively restricted to vomiting. It comes in a variety of ways. The most obvious alternative form of purging is excessive exercise, burning away the calorie intake until you eventually burn yourself away with it. This was something I did on and off but was never my vocation in purging. The main reason for this is because I just didn't have the energy most of the time. If I wasn't dozy eyed and barely able to lift my body upright as a result of prolonged starvation, then I was badly fatigued and in need of sleep after a purge. Very rarely did I have any energy at all, no matter which stage of my bulimic cycle I was in. Aside from my daily vomiting, purging also came in the form of laxatives. The objective, regardless of the method being utilised, was just to get every grain of food out of my system. When purging in the bathroom proved unsatisfactory for whatever reason, I fell back on the reassurance of laxatives, believing that anything left over would be flushed out at a rapid pace. At one point, I was taking between six to ten laxatives a day. If I ran out of them, I simply toddled down to the local pharmacy to buy them myself. No prescription required, I would purchase them with hairspray and make-up, simple.

This is just an idea of how broad the term "purging" really is and also how, many bulimics can go years without being diagnosed. What classifies someone as bulimic is too wide a context. It's one of the reasons why I have maintained, throughout my illness and also to this day, that the category should be fragmented further, to better understand one bulimic from another. But that's for a later discussion, I think.

Punishing myself – or purging, if you want to call it that – has always existed in my life. Whether physically or emotionally, the need to free myself of certain weighty feelings has always been there in one way or another.

I AM 12 YEARS old. I hate the girls in school and Mum hates them too. She says she wants to protect me and cries when she realises she can't. No matter how hard she tries, she can't protect me from those girls and this really upsets her. It has been happening for two years now and sometimes, I just wish I could die because it feels like it's never going to end.

In class, they won't sit beside me. They don't tell me why but now I always sit with the boys, who aren't as mean and they even talk to me. When we play Gaelic football, the girls never kick the ball to me and then Mr O'Brien wonders why I'm not playing. Before line-up in the mornings, they take my bag and hide it somewhere in the playground; I've been late to class a few times now and I know my teacher is getting angry with me. In the playground at lunchtime, they won't talk to me or even stand near me. I try to go over to their circle but they all move away from me and sometimes they run, laughing loudly, so everyone can see. They don't call me names like the children when I was little, but this feels much worse. I would rather they stay friends with me, even if it means being called names; this would be so much easier because at least nobody would know and besides, it's not like I don't believe what they're saying anyway.

One of the girls has started telling lies about me to the whole year. When we first came into the senior school, all the classes just stuck to themselves and didn't really play with each other. But now, in our final year of primary school, everyone knows each other so when the girls start telling lies, they tell all three classes of the year. They've told lies about me and my family too. I've overheard them talking about my mum and dad, saying disgusting things that I could never repeat. Other times, someone has told me what they're saying about me; the girls often *ask* someone to tell me, just so I know. It's mostly about my body being hairy underneath my clothes and that I smell of body odour all the time.

They go through phases with me. Despite whatever had happened before, when they welcome me back to the group, I'm always quick to return because I don't want to be the only person in sixth class without friends. When I'm around them, they tease me because I have never kissed a boy. Sometimes, I've tried to lie and tell them I have so they'll stop. But when I do this they call over all the girls from the playground, and they ask me who I've kissed and when. They ask me what it was like and say that if I really had done it, I would be able to describe it to them. Sometimes there are 12 or more girls all questioning me at once.

They recently started a rumour that I fancy a boy from a different class and now all the boys ignore me too. Sometimes even the boys come up to me in the playground and jeer me about liking various students. I deny it but that only makes it worse. Every day, I come home and am upset about something new. I cry most days now and it makes Mum really angry with those girls. I don't want to make her angry because it will just make me more upset, so I try to hide in my room when I cry. I'm so pathetic in every way and I feel too ashamed of myself to let her see. She must hate having me as a daughter.

I try my best to be better. If I could be better then maybe I wouldn't get picked on and then Mum wouldn't get upset. Being better in class doesn't count. My teacher, Mrs Behan really likes me and thinks I'm very good because I usually score high marks. But the girls jeer me even more because of it. All the popular boys are really good at sport, so I think that if I can be good at sport, everyone will like me the way everyone likes them. I'm no good at playing sports because I'm so fat, but I want to try anyway. Every year, the school holds races for all the classes and if you win, you get to compete in the local secondary school, where the fields are much bigger. I've never been very fast but this year I want to try at least.

When the day of the races comes around, we are all excused from class and taken to the field at the top of the school. I walk with the rest of the girls from my class to do the start-line of the 100 metres race. We all bend down on one knee, waiting for the whistle to blow. A hundred metres away, the entire senior school looks on before us. Everyone is watching head-on. When the whistle blows, I leap forward. I don't look around me or even think about anyone else. My gaze is fixated on the gate behind all the on lookers and my feet break against the wind before me. I'm speeding with tremendous might. Before I even realise it, I'm in 4th place. It's not 1st or 2nd or anything else of importance, but among the 15 or so girls, I'm not last anyway. Spurred onwards, I catapult forward, flailing my arms back and forth as I do so. The closer I get to the crowd, I can hear roars and cheers. It's for me, I think. I smile and laugh along with them, still pelting onwards in my stride.

As I start to see the finish line, however, I realise that they are not cheering me on. I see all the girls from other classes pointing and laughing at me, whispering to the boys beside them who then follow suit. The teachers have caught on to what's being said and look both displeased and slightly pitying. The female teachers are all snapping at the pupils and pointing their fingers, but to little avail. I don't know what is happening. I slow down, scared and unsure. In the end, I finish in 8th place, but don't care about the race anymore. I walk by all the different groups to sit down with my class. Everyone stares at me as I pass them, pointing and laughing. Finally, one of the girls I don't know roars out, 'Hey flopsy! Have you ever heard of a BRA?!' The entire congregation of students erupt into uncontrollable laughter and the girl is carted away by one of the teachers gripping her arm and shouting at her. It's not enough to stop the outbreak of hysteria among all the girls and boys.

I had never worn a bra before; I didn't think I needed to. But, being larger and slightly more developed than everyone else in my year, I had wobbly bits and bobs all over my body. During my ignorant sprint through the 100 metre race, all those forgotten bits had been wobbling and bouncing the whole way and sent everyone into a fit of giggles that caused the chaos now unfolding before me. Both the boys and girls are all falling around the place laughing and all the races have been brought to a temporary halt. I am the laughing stock of the entire year.

When school finally finishes, I am crying before I've even reached my front door. My face red and desperate and my coat wrapped tightly around my embarrassing body, I tell Mum to leave me alone and lock myself away in my room. I look in the mirror and the humiliation is still spread all over my face like dirt. I want to smash the reflection and rid myself of the person looking back. I almost black out for a moment. Everything goes still as the fury within me builds and builds. Acting of its own accord, my right hands raises itself into the air and with full force, I belt myself across the face. I'm blinded by the smack for a moment. Then I do it again, *wham!* Once more and a purple mark is appearing on my cheek. I do it again and again and again. I don't know how many times I've done it, but very suddenly the fury has passed.

I look in the mirror, humiliated and now very sore. I feel slightly better after doing this. The butt of every joke and the target of every kid in school, I deserved it for being such a freak. I burst into tears once again and curl up on my bed, holding my raw and tender cheek and cradling my wounded pride. I never want to go back to school again.

INTERVENTION

I SAT IN THE doctor's office alone. My mother, being the nervous wreck she always is – bless her heart – waited outside. She hadn't said a word to me in the car but I knew her apparent coldness was simply her way of hiding all her own nerves that I'm sure were bubbling over in her brain the entire journey. When she went to accompany me into the doctor's office, I had stretched my hand out and said, 'It's okay Mam, you wait out here.' Surprised at this and looking even more terrified than she had done first walking into the waiting room, she sat back down, no doubt convinced of the worst. We both knew what she was thinking but neither of us said it for fear of bringing up a needless conversation until we had spoken to the doctor.

We were at the doctor's office for the same concerns, but each had our own fears about what we were about to hear. I hadn't menstruated in months. My mother, too polite and accommodating for her own good to say it, thought I was pregnant; her questions about the disappearance of my period had been growing in the last number of weeks. It had finally reached a point where she was now asking me on a daily basis, 'Have you gotten your period yet?' I considered lying to her several times just to put her mind at ease but as I became more and more concerned over the matter myself, I knew I would need her to take me to a doctor at some point. So while she fretted over the possibility that her youngest daughter – only 19 years of age and still in her first year of university – could be pregnant, my thoughts ran in a completely opposite direction. It did cross my mind that being pregnant wasn't out of the question. But I just knew that this wasn't it. Call it instinct or just common sense, but I was sure that there was no way my body could be carrying a child in its current state.

It had been just over a year since all the trouble started; a year since those days spent torturing myself in the gym and almost a year since the outbreak of the dieting, the fasting, the bingeing and the purging. My body, I think, had come to a stand still. Whatever was wrong with me, it wasn't hidden anymore. Both my family and friends had confirmed this over the last number of months. But we'll look into all that momentarily.

For the time being, I sat shifting my weight from one side of the doctor's chair to the other. Barely even taking in my surroundings, all I could bring myself to do was study her as she fiddled through my files. She had greeted me in a most cheery manner, having not seen me for a very long time by that stage and apparently totally oblivious to the quiet riot that was taking place behind my eyes.

'So why are you here today?' she had asked, ever the professional but still with a welcoming tone of assurance.

'I haven't had my period in a while.' I murmured back at her, assuming she would jump to the same conclusion my mother had before. Whether or not she did, I had no idea. But it wasn't long before she confirmed that I wasn't pregnant. You would think this would have made me feel a surging sense of relief. It didn't. I knew that a girl of my age, who had experienced regular menstruation for years didn't just suddenly stop in her biological patterns for no apparent reason. Something must be really wrong with me and this is what scared me the most. The silence in the room now was too threatening for me to sit still. I stared hard at her, as if willing her to acknowledge my being in the room. *Surely she can feel the tension radiating off me*, I thought. As if she had been struck by lightning, she would suddenly realise the urgency of the proceedings at hand and put me out of my misery. Eventually, she looked up very slowly, apparently not alarmed by anything jotted down in my private medical documents.

'You've lost quite a bit of weight since the last time you were weighed here.' she finally said, indicating a recording of a little under 12 stone. I shuddered at the very sight of the figure.

'Yeah, I went on a diet,' I informed her light-heartedly.

'What was the diet?'

I gave her all the necessary details about the milkshake diet I had been on and midway through, she cut me off saying that she'd heard about it, with an air of disapproval in her voice.

'You have to be above a certain BMI and body weight for that. Did you gain a lot of weight since the last time you were weighed?'

'Err, yes,' I lied, 'the stress of my final year and all that; I gained a lot of weight.' If only she knew how I had, by contrast, been dieting and losing weight since before I even turned 18. I was suddenly uncomfortable. It was as if I was expecting something horrific to happen. This office was surely going to be the scene of a most devastating occurrence that would later be reported on the news, with a rather fat picture of me that would make me sick to look at.

Focus, I heard that voice in my head whisper. *Pay attention and keep it together. We've got this.* I believed in what she was saying fully but at the same time, was unsure about how much a person should lie to their doctor, if at all. I would take it one question at a time, I told myself. But, as it turned out I wasn't given much of a chance to do this.

'And what's your eating like now?' the doctor asked, with direct eye contact and absolutely no hesitation in her voice. Invisible chaos descended over the room and seeped into my pores, rummaging its way around the underneath of my skin. There it was. It was the question I'd been trying to answer in my own head for months, since my family and friends had started watching me with shrewd eyes. My eating was strange, yes; that was an absolutely undeniable truth. And I'd even gone as far as to call myself bulimic on many different occasions in diary entries and on my beloved pro-ED websites.

More than this, what flashed through my mind when presented with this question was not my eating or lack thereof; it was the things

I did after almost every meal now and the patterns that dominated every single day from the moment I woke up. I saw the handful of days spent without food here and there, the over the counter laxatives hidden in a box atop my wardrobe, the varying colours of my vomit painted across the toilet bowl and the weighing scales I would pull from under my bed at least 30 times a day. I felt the piercing cold that still blistered in my toes and all around my body, the build-up of plaque and grit that coated the back of my teeth, the scaly peel that laced certain areas of my skin and the throbbing aches that now riddled every joint and bone in my body. I could hear the sound of my mother's voice crying, *This isn't you, Leanne!*, the girls' words of *Leanne, you're sick* breaking through stifled tones and above all else, I could hear that familiar voice now screaming at me, *Lie! Lie to her! Lie!*

'Y-yeah' I hesitated, now evidently flustered. 'It's alright.'

She said nothing, which sent my head spinning with pressure. How much was too much to tell her? My thoughts drifted onto the issue of doctor-patient confidentiality but then dismissed the thought before returning to it again several times and each time ultimately deciding against it. Nonetheless, words started falling from my mouth like verbal diarrhoea. I wasn't sure if I was talking for the sake of telling her something or just for the sake of filling the silence that encroached like a cocoon around she and I. Whatever the reason, the words lunged from my throat faster than any purge ever had.

'Well actually, I mean, it's not perfect' I elaborated. 'I've been under a lot of pressure recently with starting college and that, so I haven't really had time to think about my eating. I am eating okay, I guess; it's just a little touch and go at the moment.'

She didn't look satisfied.

'Okay, well, my friends have all jumped to conclusions and think it's worse than it really is. But they're just being overly concerned, that's all.' I continued on like this for what felt like the bones of about ten minutes or so, digging a hole for myself and then frantically trying to pull myself back out again. Eventually, the worst had happened and I'd managed to let slip the term 'eating disorder.'

'So you're friends think you have an eating disorder?' she asked, calm as she had been when I first walked in.

'They think so, yeah.' I sighed.

'Do you think you have an eating disorder?'

I shook my head. 'No. I mean, no I don't think so.'

I thought she almost let slip a sigh. *This woman thinks I'm crazy,* I thought to myself. At the time, I think I was teetering around the ten stone mark and in that moment was fully convinced that a person of my weight could not possibly have an eating disorder, not really. One surely had to be perfectly skeletal before anyone could accuse you of having an eating disorder. Yet there I was, bound in curves and creases as I had always been, now having suggested to a doctor that I was anorexic, or whatever the term was. Within the second I had first said it, I was instantly mortified with myself.

Our conversation proved less strenuous than initially envisaged.

On the contrary, despite the many doubts that tested my ability to fully indulge in our discussion, I felt a certain ease by then. It was as if saying the term, whether it was true or not, removed a level of responsibility from me. What's more, I trusted this woman; she had a matter-of-fact way about her that shockingly did not compromise her compassion. Eventually, however, the ease of our consultation lifted and in that small office, I entered a new phase of my disease.

'Leanne,' she said, concern in her voice, 'your ovaries are giving you a clear sign that you're not getting proper nutrition. If you keep damaging your body like this, you'll find you're kidneys will be the next thing.'

'I'm not infertile or anything though, right?' I asked, panicked.

'You keep going the way you are and it's not impossible.'

I had never been a maternal person. While my girlfriends always cooed and sighed at the sight of a baby, I just never felt that internal draw that so often causes women to obsess over the idea of motherhood. I always put it down to my age. This theory came into contention when, at the premature age of 17, most of the girls around me began to show an interest in any toddler that so much as passed us with their mother.

'Oh!' they'd gasp. 'I can't wait to be a mum!'

I don't believe I have ever stated once in my young life that I even really wanted to be a mother, let alone not being able to wait for the day. I suppose, other things just seemed more important than motherhood, so it never crossed my mind to any great degree.

But when my doctor confirmed the risks I ran with my behaviours surrounding eating, something buried deep inside cried out for help. It then occurred to me that this wasn't like any measly few pounds that I could gain and lose again in a matter of days; if I could push my body to the point of losing my period altogether, there was nothing to indicate I would ever get it back. The repercussions of this tolled in my head like a bell.

I was always a little on the dramatic side. I noticed this most with matters of the heart. No matter what the circumstance or whomever the boy, if romantic intentions were put forward to me to any extent, I would automatically start weighing out every possible consequence, both positive and negative. You're probably thinking that I must scare them away almost instantly. I hardly inform such suitors of these thoughts but yes, I do have that tendency to send them running all the same. At either end of the spectrum, I would take my premonitions to every absolute extremity or possibility. As a result of this, I believe I underwent a phase of stubborn self-righteousness, as no matter what the outcome, I was always reassured that I 'just knew that was going to happen.' Furthermore, I think I always had a tendency to lean more toward the pessimistic side and usually went about my daily business convinced of the worst.

In the case of the matter at hand, the only prospect that materialised in front of me was that one day, perhaps a long time from now, I could wake up and discover that I am incapable of having children. This potential outcome, though wildly morbid and probably unlikely given that my doctor was not overly concerned about it, cast a spell over my mind for the days that followed that office exchange. For someone who had never even understood the widespread fixation with babies and the idea of having your own children, the fear of being *unable* to do so shook me to my core. It brought out in me, even if only temporarily, that most feminine spirit of all women. Greater than the jobs we worked, the clothes we strung on our backs and indeed, how thin our bodies could be, having a child was surely what defined us under the name. And if I was biologically ineligible in any way of naturally conceiving and carrying a child, I halted at the thought of there being nothing to fuel that desperately sought-after sense of definition, both as an individual and now, a woman. All at once, my friends' chatter of babies and motherhood seemed a little less silly.

Despite the very unhealthy thoughts and feelings of panic that ensued after my visit to the doctor, the effects were only short-lived. Within about four days, I was fasting again, the initial smack of fear having passed quickly. The doctor was referring me to a clinic psychologist, but I didn't have very much time to dwell on this most momentous ordeal. My weight at the time was up and down. This was something I found extremely upsetting. My disease did not guarantee weight loss and certainly it never guaranteed the physique I so obsessively coveted. Rather, it warranted an ongoing and sleepless battle of loss and gain.

There was no maintenance, you see. Even if I had attempted to maintain a particular weight, it would never have worked. If I hit my given goal weight, it was impossible to simply stay there, as I mostly saw such a pursuit as a way of giving up. More importantly, she would never allow this. She would call me weak, a quitter and a waste of clear potential. Similarly, maintaining always presented the threat of gaining. It was, in a way, just the stepping stone to the latter term. If I wasn't losing weight, I was gaining at a shocking rate. Bulimia does not take a break. It does not rest or catch up on lost sleep as you 'maintain.' I constantly went extremely one way or extremely the other. Moderation was no longer in my vocabulary, not while I shared a life with her. What this resulted in was a bombardment of various 'Leannes.' It wasn't always easy for others, I have since discovered, to tell whether I had lost or gained weight. Of course to me, if I gained as much as two pounds, it carried the weight of the world. But I marked my weight fluctuations from good to bad; eight and a half stone to ten stone and I knew people had seen the difference – mostly due to superficial compliments received from casual acquaintances and people whom I saw very little of. Ten and a half stone or above and I would refuse to leave the house. I couldn't let people see me that way. That Leanne would be locked away until she could fix herself to the point of being Miss Nine-and-a-Half Stone Leanne once more.

Along with the severe weight fluctuations, my social patterns moved along some warped meridian grid of global scope. The world would just have to revolve around me and my bulimia or else we simply would not participate in it, as was the outcome time and time again.

Plans with friends and intended outings would come about only when my bulimia dictated so. Any interactions with others were subject to her will and whether she thought I was acceptable enough to be seen. If for whatever reason I was substandard, she would convince us both of the fact and thus we would lock ourselves away in my room together, wallowing in self-loathing and that usual absence of all worth.

My self-worth was not always measured by just my weight. It extended to every facet of my aesthetical make-up. The problem was that by now – on top of all the insecurities that had existed before – my appearance had genuinely altered due to the bulimia and proved to only deepen the wound of confusion about how I looked. My hair had thinned staggeringly. Since I was a child, my mother had boasted about my locks, which were always full and bouncy even at substantial lengths. Now, it hung from my roots as if the life in it had died. With every time I washed my hair, I pulled out more and more worrying chunks. The drain would clog with the mounds falling from my head. Whereas before I had always let it flow naturally, I now found myself brushing it up, pulling, tearing and flipping it, desperate to give the illusion that there was more atop my head.

My skin was no better. Spots, sores and blisters had formed around my mouth from where my vomit-coated fingers rubbed and writhed against on a daily basis. It was rough and dry, flaking every now and then. I once owned a bearded dragon named Charlie. Like most reptiles, Charlie would shed her skin as she grew. I would go to her tank to feed her and find large pieces of skin lying on the sand, while Charlie sat like a peacock in the corner, an ever so slightly different shade in her colouring. I felt like this was happening to me now. I was shedding my skin as I had watched Charlie do for so long when she was growing. The difference was that the tint of my skin beneath was not changing to anything favourable.

'You're grey,' Anna had told me. It was during one of her relentless lectures about my health. She always used cut-throat statements; I think as a way of emphasising the severity of what she was saying. She had been one of the first to accuse me of having an eating disorder and was by far one of the most vocal of the group. 'Your skin is *grey*! Leanne, how is it even possible you can't see that?'

The truth is, I was a mixture of colours those days. Kate had commented before how my skin looked yellow, even under the usually immaculate make-up I painted over it. It was a bit of everything by that stage. Hearing Anna's voice, along with everything else that my friends had drummed into my head, I stared into the mirror, examining the splinters of skin that stuck out in random patterns. I scratched at one of them for a while, harmlessly, on the bridge of my nose. I saw some sawdust-like powder trickle down. Finally, a notable piece flaked off from the surface. I tried to get a grip on it with my now blunt index finger and thumb. My nails had stopped growing a long time ago and because I had been in the habit of biting my nails down, they were now constantly below the line of my fingertip. Eventually, I got a hold of the shard of skin. My eyes darted between my reflection and my fingers, as I tore the piece of skin right from the top and down to the bump at the bottom of my nose. It left a red and shiny slit that ran the length of my nose and stung under the exposure. My mother later gave out to me for picking at my skin when she saw both my scratched nose, as well as scabbed spots that had been bleeding only moments before.

I wonder how she would have reacted had she known what was happening inside my mouth too. My teeth, or at least the very frail impression that was left of them, ached between my gums. I started to think they were simply rotting away in my head and always feared the worst upon waking from dreams in which I discovered there wasn't so much as one tooth left. I developed a bad habit of perpetually rubbing my tongue along the inside of them, as if to test their durability or even their security to the gums from which they grew. If I pushed even remotely hard against them with my tongue, they splintered in pain. Sore to the touch, most things seemed to hurt them now and no matter what I ate during a binge, if it was anything that required chewing, it would inevitable bother my teeth in some way. Even liquids were harsh on them when too hot or cold and would heighten the sensitivity when they hit the nerves running through my mouth.

It was like one very thin thread now held them to my gums and I was sure they would fall out sooner or later with the right push or mid-way through a binge. Maybe they'd fall out while purging, unable to withstand the velocity of my own vomit. Some of them didn't feel far from it anyway. For weeks now, I was able to wedge the tip of my tongue beneath the bottom of my two front teeth. Decayed and almost dissolving away, they finished abruptly and sharply, leaving a slight gap between where they ceased and my gum began. I had gum disease as well. I knew it, even before a dentist confirmed that it was the worst form of gum disease one can get. You don't spit that much blood while brushing without there being something very problematic happening behind your lips. I wished I could do more for them; if not for their good health then even for the sake of a decent facade. I'd been a coffee drinker and smoker of about 10 to 15 cigarettes a day and now, to top it all off, had cultivated a mental resistance to mouthwash and chewing gum, both of which I knew had hidden calories. I couldn't exactly stop brushing my teeth and accepted my twice a day scrub as an unavoidable calorie intake. But I would only make room for the bare minimum, without compromising a lifetime necessity.

Along with my hair, my skin and my teeth, there was something noticeably different as a whole about me. What it was, I still find difficult to put my finger on. I carried myself in a rather contorted way; my shoulders were always hunched, my chest collapsed inwards and I forever had my arms wrapped around my abdominal area, almost nursing it and as if hiding something beneath. My mother says it was my eyes. I knew they looked a little strange, as the girls had argued on many occasions that they looked some off-coloured shade of yellow. In the months prior to writing this memoir, however, my mother broke my heart when she put it quite simply by telling me, 'You weren't there. Your eyes had no life in them anymore. It's like you just weren't there behind them.'

Whether it was my weight or any of the idiosyncrasies mentioned above, it became harder and harder to be around people. I was just too embarrassed and ashamed of what I had turned into to allow them to see me this way. Some sociable activities were unavoidable, such as birthdays and generally just proving I still existed. But these events were usually agonised over and sent me into a tornado of fasting and purging, attempting recklessly to lose weight even if just for the one night. When I did have to show my face, I was relatively chatty, lively and cool natured. The need for secrecy meant I had to be. I have found this to be true of most bulimics I have spoken with. The fabrication of what you are and the reality are two entirely different people. Hiding the reality was of the utmost importance, as just one night of glory could fuel me to struggle on for weeks thereafter, a refreshed objective in further charging my disease.

The truth is, for all my invented perceptions and lively countenance, I believed I was dying inside, if not completely dead and buried already. The worst part was that nobody even knew it, not fully. They couldn't have, because it was only I who lingered in that desolated cave of my mind. Bulimics are very often contradictory in this way; they can be social creatures and lead lives of total normality –

quite well, might I add – and yet, remain some of the loneliest people inhabiting this earth. The loneliness I endured during that time of my life is something I hope never to experience again.

It's more than just the feeling of being isolated. I was disconnected mentally, physically and emotionally from the entire human race, it seemed; I didn't even feel part of it. I was a subspecies of the people who walked the streets and went about their daily lives. I was not part of the world they'd built and lived in. I was like a half-formed variety of what they were; a critter that was intended to be like them but was never finished. I was unworthy of the space I took up in that world and the lies I showcased in order to fit in. At long last, I was the living rendition of the monster that lived in my reflection. It was this realisation that sucked me deep into that bottomless vat of depression.

In bed at night was when I felt it the most. A hole had been carved in me and was growing bigger by the day. The physically overwhelming emptiness caused by fasting and purging had permeated right to all seeds of emotion, killing them away. I would have chosen uncomplicated sadness over this; sadness at least retained some purity and a confirmation of some emotion. I would have chosen anything but this. The sensation hurt like hell. That's where I was and I'd known it for a long time now; I was in hell. I just knew I would die here and when that time came to pass, I would be alone. Even she would have abandoned me by then.

I AM 15 YEARS old. I'm walking down a long corridor in Dublin's Mater Hospital. I've never been here before because nobody has ever mattered so much to me that I should visit. From the outside, the hospital resembles something along the lines of a university or state building, perhaps. Amidst beautiful grounds of well-kept grass and flourishing flowers, there sits the Mater itself. It has an overbearing presence about it. Though intimidating, it holds in its stance an air of architectural magnificence, as if concealing something truly spectacular from the world in which it dwells.

The only ominous thing about this place is the steps, which run high and very wide, leading you into its heart. The pillars that rest above those steps blockade its front door. They are almost frightening and resemble a stone cage that could hold the biggest and most dangerous of all beasts. As I get a little closer to them, I think how a terrifying monster must live here, deep within the walls.

Inside is a mishmash of old and new; mahogany wood panelling colliding with steel-like floors and desks. It feels wrong, like the original purpose of the place has been compromised somehow and has resulted in an offensive distortion. Very suddenly, I don't trust this place and I don't want to be here anymore. It scares me almost as much as the thought of why I am here in the first place.

I'm sitting in a chair that has been designated to me, beside an open door where light spills out into the hallway. This must be the old part of the building. It's very dark for a hospital and boasts statue after statue of various saints whose names I can't remember. Fear grips me and glues me to my seat, as I chew away at my nails and tear at the

176

skin around my cuticles. The room spilling out light is quiet, with soft murmurs drifting their way into the hallway. The priest was in there today, I was told. I don't dwell on this fact and forget it the moment I remember it. I don't want to think about how many people have died in that room or in that bed. The thought makes me cower slightly and all my childhood fears of ghouls and ghosts are instantly sparked up again. Just as I think I'll burst out of my seat and run crying down the hallway and back out to the beautiful gardens, it's my turn to go into the room. I take a deep breath and then hold it for as long as I can.

The decor of the hallway, which resembled that of a church, has abruptly disappeared and been replaced by cold steel and pale blue bed sheets. The room has that clinical smell that only a hospital can have. My sister is weeping and I can tell she is suppressing a somewhat violent sob. All the sombre faces attempt to refigure themselves into faces of assurance. They fail but I appreciate the effort nonetheless. All eyes are on me, my gaze falls upon the hospital bed and I well up with emotion, a heavy lump in my throat and a cold dampness over my heart.

My father smiles at me from his steel bed. I hardly recognise the man bar that smile, which I've seen a thousand times before. There are wires everywhere, running in and out of him. On the other end of each wire, is connected to one or more of the ugly machines that flash bright lights and make beeping and buzzing sounds.

'You okay, babe?' he asks in a voice that does not belong to my father. I nod uncertainly. I have no words.

I have a very vague recollection of the day my father was struck by a heart-attack. At the time, I had no idea of the severity. He had suffered with heart related problems before, including something called Bell's palsy, which made one side of his face drop completely for a while. But this was different because he had never looked like this before. Mum had warned me that Dad wouldn't look 'too great' and that a quadruple bypass was a very big ordeal. If only I had known what she meant then; perhaps I wouldn't be so struck with horror now. I don't know how my face looks because I've lost all sensation in it. It can't look very pleasing because everyone around me resumes whatever conversation they were having before I entered the room. They're talking about the priest from today, but I zone out from the conversation.

My father was a man who prided himself on a clean shave. I remember as a child that he had boasted a full beard and for a time, just a moustache. As I'd gotten older though, he was always well-shaved and I never saw so much as one bit of stubble on his face. He was a tidy man and kept everything about him very neat. But he isn't tidy now and his dishevelled appearance causes me to think the worst. He is half-slumped back on the pillows, too weak to fully lift himself. His salt-and-pepper hair, usually shaved down to a very fine blade, looks almost shaggy now. I can definitely run my fingers through it if I try. I can't remember ever doing that. His face, now gaunt around the eyes and with hollowed cheeks, has not been shaved in quite a while and grey stubble laces his jaw from ear to ear. His skin has turned a soured cream colour and because of this, his dark brown eyes – the ones he has passed down to me – look big and heavy, as if it is a struggle for his face to even hold them in place, never mind keep them open.

I exchange glances with my sister. When her eyes meet mine, she fills up with tears again. She knows what I'm thinking because out of everyone in this room, she knows me best and can read me like a book. I can't stand to look at her too long for fear of crying in front of everyone. Along with my aunt and uncle, my dad's twin is also here. This is in addition to my mother, sister and brother. I have to hold it in for the time being at least. Besides, I'm distracted by the fresh scars I can see on my father's body. His hospital gown is thrown awkwardly around him and falling off a little.

Poor Mum, I think to myself. *She clearly tried to tidy him up for us.* When it's time to leave, I feel a wounding thrash of guilt because in truth, I don't want to be here anymore. I shouldn't want to leave my Dad here all alone but I just can't stand to be in this room anymore and I simply can't stand to look at him any longer. One by one, we give him a hug and a kiss goodbye. I don't want to hug him because I'm afraid of hurting him in some way. And when I kiss his cheek I want to cry because I have never kissed his cheek; he always kisses mine and it hurts me to know he physically can't bring himself to do it right now.

Mum tries to approach the topic gently but you can only be so delicate with such matters before you merely obstruct the truth. She tells us that they're not sure if Dad will make it and that she wants us to be prepared for the worst. That's why the priest was there, I finally realise Dad was receiving the last rights.

As we make our way down the steps outside the hospital, I find that I suddenly hate this building. I want to kick it and spit on it for lying. Looking so beautiful on the outside, it stands as a lie to what really happens inside its walls. The beast that it cages is death and it hides it in that superficial beauty I first believed in. Within those walls lies our biggest fear. I saw it all over my father's face. At the sight of him on that bed, I knew that what people fear the most is our own mortality. My father was now trapped in that fear, hidden behind these walls. He was living inside the beast.

Lying in bed, I can't sleep. I have never felt this way before. It is the purest emotion I have ever experienced and roars inside me like a train. My chest feels tight and a dark cloud has descended over me. This is what sadness truly is. It is raw, invasive and unrelenting. I cry myself to sleep, hoping I won't feel this sadness again when I wake.

I REMEMBER VERY LITTLE of that chapter in my life. The events prior to this memory and after it have surpassed a point of haziness and just don't seem to exist anymore. My family can't understand how I have memories from as young as five but cannot remember something from the age of 15. My father made a full recovery over time but still, I remember nothing of it. I have tried very hard but it seems everything surrounding this one memory has been lost in the archives of my memory. I don't think I'll ever know what happened in that time. But that day I visited my father in hospital remains a pivotal moment of my young life. It was the first time, I believe, that I truly felt the sensation of raw sadness. It was the most potent emotion I had ever experienced. I thought nothing could be worse than that, until I lost the capacity to feel more or less anything. My eating disorder caused me to slip into a deep depression and I remember during that time wishing I could once again feel the purity of human emotion, even sadness. I have never forgotten either sensation.

In the weeks that lead up to that faithful doctor's appointment, my life – as well as the one I also shared unrestrictedly with my bulimia – entered a stage of complete turmoil. For one thing, the academia I once prided myself on and defined myself by, fell to shambles. The transition from secondary school to university had proved to be an extremely emotional upheaval. Everyone had talked to such extraordinary lengths about the difficulties in this changeover; so much so, that it almost felt too cliché to admit that I was struggling very badly. On a very basic level, I simply found that I could not keep up with the workload. In school, I had been top of my class in most subjects. Assignments were carried out with efficiency, as well as to a high standard. But in the realms of that campus and all the university had to offer, I found myself utterly lost.

Schoolwork had always consisted of studying facts and writing about them. Its demands extended only as far as regurgitating what you have read onto a page. My school had been in walking distance of my family home and I found a great deal of comfort in both the uniform which we wore every day – free from the inconvenience of having to select clothes each morning and unifying us in school spirit – as well as the Monday to Friday hours that had been so familiar for six years. In university, the demand for independent study reached new levels I had never before experienced. It was more than the study of facts and I think I began to panic right from the beginning when I realised that much of what I would learn in this place would have to be self-taught.

Most days, I barely made it to the campus, lecture halls or the shelved abyss they called the library. Indeed, I barely made it out of bed. The mornings were the worst; I had always been an early riser and while my peers struggled to wake before 1.00 pm, I always found I could never sleep far past 9.00 am. So by every measure, waking for college in the mornings should have been as easy as it had always been. But upon waking, I suffered something more than just the run of the mill tiredness, my body felt like it had been physically arrested by the might of lethargy and malnutrition. I would lie there with my eyes open, watching the clock as the minutes ticked by. I was not fighting sleep or anything else that would tempt most others to remain wrapped up beneath the covers; I simply couldn't move. My legs and arms were weighed down by invisible chains. No matter how much weight I lost, I just could not lift my body up from the mattress. I felt like the pinnacle of where all the earth's gravity travelled to. I was submerged under that weight and could not rise.

'Are you going to college today, Leanne?' my mother would ask from the door. To say she was concerned at this point was an understatement. More than my physical appearance and the changes in my personality she had witnessed and commented on regularly, she became most fearful with the development of my apparent lack of interest in my studies. This was not like me and could only be the result of something entirely horrendous. Sometimes it was as simple as telling her that a lecture had been cancelled, my timetable had been changed or just that this morning's lecture wasn't important at all. But on other occasions, I did not possess even the mental capacity to do this.

'No, I'm not,' is all I would say; end of discussion. She would hover at the door a while, silently expressing both her disapproval and her undeniable worry. I didn't care. If she felt what my body was feeling, she would leave me alone and not question my decision. Besides, I knew that even if I managed to physically present myself in the lecture theatres on campus, I would not be fully there anyway. If I wasn't sleeping somewhere in the back, I would be scrawling notes at a very slow pace, mentally incapable of digesting what was being said because my brain was just working at too slow a pace to keep up. This was not the kind of student I was and I suppose somewhere in the back of my mind, I just thought it was a temporary phase that would pass once I became comfortable in my new surroundings. The problem was that I just couldn't get comfortable here; I'd never known university without an eating disorder and it affected my perceptions of the place greatly. Everything about college became related to an ongoing sense of difficulty and a feeling of forever being behind.

More than this, the hardest thing in my transition from secondary school into third level education was having to accept how truly average I was. I had always excelled in one way or another and it defined me in my own head under certain terms as being a person who just did well instinctively. I was top of the class by nature, not nurturing. This had been who I was. Now, however, I was cast into a system whereby my student number was more recognisable than my own name. There was nothing about who I was that classified me as any different or any better than any other person in a lecture hall. In such a large group, I was guaranteed of the fact that many others were better than me. How I qualified what was 'better' came in a variety of forms; smarter, prettier, more dedicated, more ambitious, better dressed, or wealthier. It didn't matter which because all it amounted to was that, whoever they were, they were a better version of me. What all this culminated to was feelings of total insufficiency and pressing mediocrity. Being average, as I then realised I had always been, further instilled the idea of my own worthlessness both in academia and in general.

The effect my bulimia would ultimately have on my studies was monumental. It drove away all ambition and more importantly, hindered my potential. Missing classes and lectures as a result of overpowering exhaustion was only part of it. It was like my brain had slowed down; like somebody had cut off the oxygen being fed to it and the cells had started to die off one by one. Processing information seemed an impossible endeavour. When it came to assignments, presentations or whatever else was being asked of me, I found that I simply could not mentally grasp the task at hand. It was beyond my scope and understanding by that time. This terrified me. I knew then that I had truly lost myself to my bulimia. We did not share a life anymore because if this was the case, holding on to what had always been of colossal significance would have remained a priority. No, 'sharing' was not in her vocabulary and instead, she now owned my life entirely. Along with my health, my personality, my faith and my happiness, she had now taken my education. It was among the saddest losses during my time being sick. To lose my education was to truly lose myself.

As time continued to drag on, the changes I experienced were of prodigious proportions in my life then and what it would go on to become. The biggest change occurred in my relationship with bulimia. Relationships, regardless of their context or the parties involved, revolve around a level of commitment from both sides. I was committed to my bulimia in a way that I had never been committed to anyone before. And yet, the dynamics of our relationship underwent a period of evolution in which it transformed to a commitment of absolute hatred. I had loved her once, I was sure of it. But during the course of a period that has since become the most blurred and distorted of my memories, I began to question her. This was the first step on a road which would ultimately lead me to hate her. And hate her I did. Her voice was no longer a source of comfort or encouragement or even reassurance. It was now a cage that kept me trapped in my own mind. It was the madness that now consumed my entire life and from which I could not escape. After a while, I sincerely thought I had gone mad.

For all this hatred and regret, however, I could not bring myself to destroy her. I could not be without her and for the life of me, I just couldn't understand why. It didn't matter how much we hated each other now – yes, she hated me with the same fervour and passion – because she remained the lifelong friend to whom I was tied to psychologically, spiritually, physically and emotionally. She was my friend. Life without her would surely be no life at all.

I AM 12 YEARS old. Valentine's Day is one of the days I dread the most every year. When it comes around, Mum sends me a Valentine's card in the post and then pretends that it's not from her. When I was little, I genuinely believed I had a secret admirer because everyone played along. Then when I was a little bit older, Natalie had said to me, 'You know they're always from Mum, right?' I remember feeling deceived and as if everyone pitied me and so, had it out with my Mum. She never sent me a card again.

What I dislike most about Valentine's Day is when it falls on a weekday because everyone in school has to make a card during arts and crafts. Nobody really makes a card for anybody in particular but I don't like doing it all the same because it reminds me of being little when everyone gave them to each other. I would never get a card and was embarrassed the entire day. Though we have to make our own cards, a boy in the class named John has brought in a real one from a shop. It's white with a heart on the front and kisses along the interior. It looks as though someone put on loads of red lipstick and kissed the page from top to bottom. It hasn't been written on and he says it's not for anybody and that he doesn't know why he has it. Now that it's lunchtime, a few people take an interest in the card. We only have about ten minutes in the classroom before it's yard time.

There's a boy in my year called Emmet. Everyone in school knows I like him, including Emmet himself. When the girls in my class see that John has brought a real Valentine's card today, they start to tell me that I should give John's card to Emmet. I don't want to because I know everyone will laugh at me if I do.

'Nobody will laugh at you,' one of the girls tell me. 'It's Valentine's Day; it's what you're *supposed* to do.'

But I'm still not convinced. It's a Friday and the school bullies have been nice to me this week. I don't want this to end. Sometimes they decide they want to be friends with me and I am always grateful when they do because then everyone else is nice to me as well. I'm afraid not to do what they say because they might stop being friends with me again and then next week will be horrible. They tell me that it's not like anything bad is going to happen and that it's the end of the week anyway.

'If something goes wrong,' one interjects, 'you won't be in school until next Monday so it will be forgotten by then.'

'Nothing will go wrong anyway,' exclaims another, clearly impatient now. Since 5th class, she has been what Mum calls the 'ringleader' and when she says this, everyone is in agreement.

'Besides, don't you think it will be nice for Emmet to get a Valentine's card? I mean, you do like him don't you?'

I nod, afraid of the implications of this admission.

'Well then,' she continues, 'this will make him like *you*. You just have to do it now or else you'll never know.'

Still unsure of what to do, I take the card from John, who looks nervous for me now. It's not like he can say anything against the girls anyway but deep down, I appreciate his evident concern. I remove the card from its plastic covering and open it up, looking at all the kisses running down the inside of it. Whoever made this must have really liked kissing.

'Well go *on!*' the ringleader insists. I take the pen in my hand and shakily, scribble down on the card:

To Emmet,

Happy Valentine's Day.

From, Leanne.

I write his name on the envelope and just as I'm about to tuck the card away into the paper, the girls around me start demanding to see what's written and telling me to stop hiding it. Even John is interested now to see what I have written and rather suddenly, the card has been snatched from my hand.

'That's crap!' shouts the ringleader. 'You didn't even put in any kisses.'

'You have to put kisses in at the end, otherwise it doesn't really count,' another informs me. I refuse and try to grab the card back out of her hand. I'm not quick enough and the other girls form some kind of human wall around her.

'I'll put them in for you, if you're too chicken to do it', she bellows. I knew this was a bad idea. I want to go back just two minutes in time and not take that pen in my hand. I have a lump in my throat and am scared of what's going to happen. The girls are all smiling broadly with those dangerous smiles that always set off alarm bells in my chest. By now, most of the boys have taken interest too and are laughing at top volume. There is no teacher in the classroom to protect me and give out to them because all the teacher's are on their break, with someone walking the halls to keep all the classes in order. I pray in my head that they will walk into our classroom, tell everyone to sit back down in their seats and to stop messing.

I watch as one scratches two kisses beneath my name on the card. Then she shouts, 'Look! She put kisses in and everything,' to the rest of the class, holding the card up high like a golden trophy. I feel flustered and then I snap at her, telling her to stop messing around.

'Oh relax,' one tells me, 'we're only having a bit of fun. Why are you such a buzz kill?'

'It's okay, Leanne,' the ringleader announces, 'I'll give the card to Emmet.'

'No.' I say, not even stopping to think. A knowing look of insult flashes across her face.

'Why not? I'm trying to do you a favour here. Are you telling me you're going to walk up to him yourself and give it to him?'

'No,' I mumble.

'Right, well then it's settled. I'll give it to him when we go outside.'

When the second bell rings and everyone starts to shuffle their way out the door, I'm already sick to my stomach. I had a five minute wait before lunchtime was over and it had felt like hours, giving my tummy time to curdle and my anxiety to catch every organ in my body and set them alight. I haven't said a word or touched any of my food. I want all this to stop now but know it's too late, everything is out of my power and there's nothing I can do. I trot outside the classroom and make my way to the yard. I can see Emmet up ahead of everyone laughing and joking with his friends.

I'm going to be the butt of that joke soon, I think to myself.

When we're finally outside, I sit down on the curb with a few of the girls from my class. They're all buzzing about the card but I'm not saying a word. Eventually, one of the girls finally seems to notice me for the first time, as if I had just walked over a moment ago.

'Oh Leanne,' she says, 'so I'm going over with the card now, okay?'

Everyone giggles. I don't reply. I wish I could sink into the gravel at my feet and stay there until all this has passed.

'*HELLO?*' she insists.

'Yeah, okay,' I say under my breath. With that, herself and another girl start trotting off across the yard; they're giddy and nearly hysterical as they leave. Most of the boys are playing football in an empty space in the middle of the yard. I watch as the two approach Emmet mid-match. There seems to be a moment of confusion when all the boys notice what's happening. A crowd encircles them and soon enough, roars and howls can be heard echoing all around them, bouncing from the concrete walls all the way over to the church beside us. All the boys are laughing, while one of the girls continues to talk to Emmet, who looks down at the card in his hands with a blank expression.

Some apparently outrageous comment is passed and sets the cluster of people off into chaos. While the boys start hopping around Emmet, thumping him on the back, the ringleader glances back at me with a threatening glint in her eye. I'm frantic now and look to Emmet's face; I can't tell if he's smiling or laughing. All I can see is that his cheeks have flared red. He stretches out his arm and tries to give the card back to the girls from my class and that lump in my throat is huge now. I want to cry. The ringleader puts her hands up, refusing to accept it and then she hurries back to the rest of the girls and I on the curb. One or two of the boys from a different class follow. Emmet stuffs the card in his back pocket, still red faced, shoving all the boys off him and eventually resumes his football game.

'What did you say?' I ask them upon their return. It's all I can think about.

'Nothing, relax,' she replies. She's lying. I know she is. Within moments of the lie falling from her mouth, however, a boy called

Luke runs up and makes a sudden halt in front of me. Luke is one of Emmet's friends.

With no warning, he blurts out, 'Is it true you *actually* did all those kisses on that card?' Horror descends over me. One of the bullies had told everyone that I had put on lipstick and kissed all over the inside of the Valentine's card.

'No!' I fret. 'No, I didn't! It's just the design.'

'Liar,' Luke laughs.

'I'm not lying! Rub the card and you'll see, it's just the design on it.'

'As *if* anyone's going to touch where your lips have been!'

With this last statement, Luke and the other boys stroll away, holding one another up as they laugh. Yet again, I am the laughing stock of the entire year. I want to stand up and scream at these girls for making me do this and for lying to all the boys about the kisses on the card. But I remain on the ground, afraid that if I stand too quickly the adrenaline I feel now will fade and I'll crumble and maybe even cry.

'Why did you lie to them?' I demand.

'Oh Jesus,' she says, rolling her eyes, 'you're no fun at all. We're only joking, have a sense of humour.'

This is the end of the discussion and I know it. If I push the matter any further, she and I will have a fight and then the girls won't talk to me for ages. That's the last thing I need now. When it's time to go inside, I'm relieved to finally leave the yard. As we walk to the classroom, all the boys are still hooting and laughing at me. While

Emmet shuffles as fast as he can down the corridor and out of sight, his face still blooming pink as he goes. The walk down the corridor had seemed so long and when I finally sit down, I think I can't feel any worse than this.

A girl from my class called Shauna walks over to me. She's a nice girl who is very quiet but doesn't pick on me. I look up to her and she awkwardly whispers, 'Ehm, Leanne, you know that card you got off John? Well, I thought I should tell you, he brought it into school today for *you.*'

My heart plummets with guilt and regret. Not only had I let the girls make a fool out of me again, I had given away my very first Valentine.

'Leanne, are you coming out with us this weekend?' one of the girls asks later during class time. I don't answer because I can't bring myself to talk to her. I can see it all over her face how much this irritates her and I'm scared again.

'Leanne,' she repeats. 'We're still friends aren't we?'

'Yeah.' I mutter.

'So you're coming out with us this weekend then?'

'Yeah, I am.'

I AM VERY FORTUNATE to have always kept diaries from a very young age. They are usually forgotten until once in a blue moon, I may choose to take a trip back through the nostalgia of my past. It's ironic; the many times I have read back through diary entries about these girls, I have cursed myself blind. I tell myself that I was a foolish girl for not seeing them for the bullies they were and for not refusing their friendship. And yet for all my self-righteous hindsight, the patterns of history seem forever destined to resurface and replay all over again. My relationship with bulimia during my teens wasn't that much different to my relationship with these girls.

I both hated and feared my bulimia as I had done with those girls so many years ago. Yet in both cases, I simply could not bring myself to refuse them or let them go. No matter how much my bulimia or those children hurt me, I would always return to them when they called, unable to push them away. It's difficult now to interpret what psychological mentality I was operating under – both at the age of 12 and again at 18 – to constantly surround myself with people and environments that would hurt me. It seemed a lot of the time I chose to do this. Sometimes I think over that issue of self-worth when I think back on such things. When it came to all the hurt, all the self-loathing and humiliation, deep down I think I chose these things because I felt it was what I deserved.

Under this logic, the most venomous thing in my life has always been me. I was my own worst enemy, choosing to envelope myself with things and people who I knew would cause me pain in some way. It was as if this punishment somehow acted as justification to my very existence, which for the most part, felt unwarranted. I was a prisoner of my own self-destructiveness and I could trace the pattern back years.

By the age of 18, however, some of the pattern had been broken; or at the very least, simply transformed into new methods of self-abuse like bulimia. You see, though I battled a raging eating disorder in the labyrinth of my mind, I was blessed to have the most devoted group of friends. I met most of these people around the ages of 14 and 15. The repercussions of the social misery I experienced before that point would have an immeasurable impact on my life in later years. But after that age at least, I would never again suffer what I had before at the hands of the people I called friends. The friends I met in my early teens were extraordinary souls who brought out the very best in me, while always accepting the very worst without judgement. I never knew people like this existed until that time. I was dazzled by them and forever in awe. To this day, such feelings retain that same tenacity as before and our bonds have been strengthened over the years. They were and always will be the collective heroes of this story.

However, prior to the day of my aforementioned doctor's visit, it had been weeks since I'd spent a decent amount of time with my friends. I knew they were questioning my absence but no longer even had the energy or the notion to care. Something inside me had changed and I had let them go along the way. I had forgotten why we were friends and more worryingly, I had forgotten why I needed them so much. They knew about my eating disorder long before I ever did and had individually used the term in their many outbursts surrounding the issue. What's more, they hated it with such a passion that I sometimes wondered if that person in my mind cowered from them in fear. Looking back now, a part of me hopes she did cower.

While that's very easy to say now, of course the matter was an entirely different thing then. They became annoyances in my life. They were people I had to hide from and lie to because if I didn't, they would give me and my secret 'friend' a whole world of trouble. In order to keep her safe, I had to distance myself from my friends as much as possible. Indeed, I think I lost a friend or two along the way; a regret that still lingers over me today. You would think – as I was convinced would happen – after so many arguments about my eating, so many tears and so many failures, that these people would eventually give up the fight and leave me in the depths of my disease. But they didn't. In fact, they clung to me like glue, as if letting me go even slightly would cause me to slip through their fingers. In fact, their presence in my life was most apparent at the times I least wanted it, the times *she* saw it as inconvenient. They threatened her so much because above anything else, my friends were the constant living proof that I could care for something more than I cared for her.

One of the biggest turning points in my illness came with a simple phone call. The girls had arranged a lunch in one of their houses. Like everyone else, I agreed to join them. But when the minutes starting ticking closer and closer to the hour, uncontrollable trepidation set in. If I went, I would most certainly have to eat, as what person attends a lunch and doesn't eat it? Coming home to purge would be no good because my mother would be home by that time and certainly question what would then be my second shower of the day. I contemplated trying to purge straight away after the lunch by excusing myself from the table, but knew that my friends were now watching me too closely for that. No, it had to be avoided completely.

I rang to say I couldn't make it because I wasn't feeling too well. It was an exhausted excuse by now but was all that came to mind in the moments of internal hysteria. They said they would come up to see me instead and naturally – perhaps even too hastily – I refused point blank. Something was different about this phone call. The tone of voice on the other end was wrong somehow and while chatting to just the one person, I could detect sounds of consternation and alarm in the background chatter. I hung up as soon as possible, slipping back onto the sofa with my empty stomach and comfortable in the knowledge that I could sleep until my mother came home.

When the unexpected knock came at the door, I didn't hear it because along with everything else, my hearing seemed to be numbing away. But when the doorbell rang throughout the house, waking me up with an electric shock. Agitated by the abrupt awakening from my post-purge coma, I knew things were going to get worse when I opened the door to my friends. They said very little, as if afraid I would shut the door in their faces and instead bustled their way past me and into the sitting room. Confused and somewhat resentful about what I interpreted as utter rudeness, I sat down with them in the sitting room, a cold look darkening my wearied face.

'I know you said not to come up, but we had to,' one of them said.

'We're not here to have lunch, we're here to talk to you. If we don't intervene now, we're scared of what's going to happen.'

'Okay,' I hesitated, the indignation still evident in my expression. 'What's going on?'

'Leanne, you have a problem and we need to talk about it,' said another.

I already knew it before they had said it. This was about my eating and I was about to be set upon by five or six women. I took a deep breath, but nothing could have prepared me for that moment when finally, there was no escaping what they were about to say.

'Leanne,' one of the girls sighed. 'You have an eating disorder. And we think you know it's true as well as we do.'

The conversation that erupted at the utterance of this statement was the scariest and most overwhelming of my entire life. In the thick of it, my friends went on to claim that I had lost a great deal of weight and was, in their opinion at least, emaciated. They told me I was sick and that I needed help. They said I wasn't myself anymore; that not only did I look different, but that my sickness had changed me as a person too. I wasn't the friend most of them met so many years ago. A number of them welled up as they talked about how they couldn't watch their friend starve and vomit her way into a hospital bed or worse, into the grave. They interrogated me over and over, relentlessly pushing for the admission that what they needed. They didn't get it, not fully anyway. I saw the pain in their eyes and heard the exhaustion in their words. It was the first time I ever realised how far down into my own darkness I had brought them.

Something snapped inside me for the worst. I was scared, cornered and under a wave of guilt for what I had done and was still doing to them. I had made their lives, as I had made my own, a living hell. The demons I battled with overpowered me in that moment and I took the cruellest action I think I ever could have. I laughed at them.

They were right in one way though; I had long since admitted to myself that I had an eating disorder. But overcoming denial is a slow process. I could admit that I had a problem to myself, but I still felt the need to conceal it from them, despite the fact that they knew everything anyway. If I admitted it to them, my control over this situation would be gone completely and I couldn't cope with that. Since that time, however, I have never forgotten the looks on their faces; the tiredness, the desperation, the hurt, the tears and most of all, the concerned expressions that are imprinted all over my memory of that day. On the surface, my friends' emotional intervention had very little impact. It would be weeks before I ever went into the doctor's office and for a while, it even drove me further away from them. Yet the consequences of our actions are not always immediately apparent. It can take a very long time for the effects of such events to show themselves. I recall months later, breaking down into tears with the mysterious burden that hung in my chest about that day. Remembering it all with ferocious accuracy, I wept hopelessly with one thought: *I'm so sorry.*

The truth is, whether it was the late night phone calls, the long-winded talks that would drag on for hours at a time, the shared tears, the endurance of listening to my suicidal thoughts, or simply the many cups of tea that were made; these women, in so many ways, saved my life time and time again. We are a sisterhood of sacrosanct devotion and love that I will be happily indebted to for the rest of my days. I owe these women my life.

RECOVERY

COMING TO TERMS WITH your past is one of the most difficult things a person can do in their life. Subconsciously, most of us fear our past; not only is it often filled with mistakes and regrets, but it also stands as proof to the fact that time – our ever looming enemy in this life – is still moving at a rapid pace. Our past is a reminder of how our present will also soon leave us and how the things we do now will fall into that vague realm of our own history. We will analyze that history at some future point under the glory of hindsight and think to ourselves, *why?* The pages of time are long and heavy to bear unless deeply understood and more importantly, reconciled with. More than this, our past is sometimes the only tool we may utilize in predicting our future. And if it is one of regret, we could certainly fall into a paralysis of utter despair and hopelessness.

These were just some of my fears throughout my months of therapy. I didn't want to look at myself that closely or the past that had come to define me. But what came about in that period of time was a regenerated outlook on the issue of my yesteryears and their significance in shaping the idiosyncratic features of my disease. It was during that time I realised that even the memories we so desperately endeavour to repress can prove to be our greatest comrades as we move in to the future. A renewed concept of hope was born. And as it turns out, hope is the most powerful artillery we can ever use against the frontiers of our own fear.

Inevitably, I resisted recovery to the best of my ability. My doctor had referred me to a clinical psychologist and, not wanting to undermine the suggestion, I went along with it just for the sake of keeping everyone happy. I knew it would be something that would ease the concerns of my interfering friends for a while. In my head, attending the weekly sessions meant a greater stretch of freedom to actually continue with my destructive behaviours. I figured if I could just do what everyone wanted of me, they would eventually realise that it wasn't working and leave me be, accepting the fact that I would never change and that my bulimia would be a part of me until the day I died.

I didn't tell my family though and it would be about a quarter of the way through my time in therapy before they ever discovered I was taking such measures. You see, unlike my friends, my family had never applied a term to what was wrong with me. They never made outward accusations surrounding my eating habits and my dramatically altered personality. My mother, prior to the writing of this memoir told me, 'I just couldn't find the words. It was obvious something was really wrong; you just weren't right. I knew you were sick, I just didn't know what to call it.' I knew this at the time and though I was aware it would have certainly reassured both of my parents to know that I was getting help, I refused to tell them in case they too came to the same conclusion my friends had. Whether or not they believed I had an eating disorder was irrelevant; as long as they didn't say it, I could continue to enjoy the comforts of home.

This will be simple, I thought. If anything, it was surely going to assist me in the secrecy of my bulimia. I just had to talk to a stranger once a week and it would be enough to convince the people around me that I was 'fixed', thus enabling me to start afresh in the life I tried so hard to keep hidden from the world. Looking for the silver lining was never my forte, as I've always been a pessimist, but when this situation was apparently unavoidable. Nevertheless, I resisted my belief in this new development. In life, you generally only get out what you put in and I assumed that these weekly sessions could only affect me if I allowed them to. It was just one more thing I could control in my own mind. So under this logic, I built a fort under which I could bury myself and as such, keep the influence of this stranger and the ammunition she may have at a comfortable distance.

Yet for all my arrogance and audacity, I was a nervous wreck on my first day. I sat down for the first of many times in front of an open-faced woman with an air of absolute surety about her. Her name was Michelle and there was nothing even remotely threatening in her general disposition. But what she represented was enough to wrack me internally. I didn't like her, I was sure of it. Still unable to admit I had a problem, my friend Ami accompanied me into her office. While I explained in broken plot lines why I was there, Ami served to fill in the gaps and finish with, 'Basically, it's very clear that Leanne has an eating disorder and we think it's gotten to the stage where she needs to talk to a professional about it.' Apparently not swayed by either of our words, my anxiety was met with unnerving calmness from this woman.

She doesn't believe me, is all I could think. *I'm too fat to have an eating disorder and this woman thinks I'm lying through my teeth.*

With Ami having been excused from the meeting at the request of the calm woman who looked at me with shrewd eyes, I decided that I would not come back. It was that simple. This was pointless and once again, I was unsure of why I was even here. The question of whether or not I truly had an eating disorder had bounced back and forth in my head for far too long to remain undecided. Yet here I was believing once again that I was perfectly fine, after writing the words 'I know I have an eating disorder' in a diary entry only the day before. Whether or not I did, I was sure that being here was not going to help me answer the question.

As the conversation progressed, however, I found a degree of warmth in her. Though I was still hell bent on handling this situation on my terms and my terms alone, I couldn't help being drawn in ever so slightly by the way in which she spoke, the fortitude with which she upheld herself and the confidence in the things she was saying.

Furthermore, I noted somewhere in my mind, a distinct lack of falsity as regards this environment. There was no couch for me to lie on, no glasses resting on the very tip of her nose, no haughty bookcase full of unrecognisable titles and no pretentiously clichéd questions such as, 'And how did that make you *feel?*' The space was small and private, almost as well hidden as the complexities of my relationship with my bulimia. It felt oddly familiar and like something I could keep in my pocket if I so wished. I left knowing only two things; the first was that I would not return next week and it would be as simple as blowing off my friends, which I did very often now; the second, was that she wasn't all that bad.

Familiarity is something most human beings are determined to establish in any situation. Without it, we cannot attain that life goal of complacency, which we convince ourselves is necessary in the pursuit of happiness. Like so many others, I was naturally resistant to any imposed change that was beyond my own control. It would mean that I was required to work much harder in any route I took to that holy grail of happiness that we each seek in our own ways. The environment Michelle provided for me and indeed, the natural demeanour of the woman herself, did offer at least some ounce of acquaintance. However, the reasoning that had brought me here still embodied that air of alteration that I felt I just wasn't ready for.

It's a very fortunate thing that – for whatever reason, which I don't fully recall – I did return the following week because I sincerely doubt I ever would have been 'ready' for it. It wouldn't have mattered whether this change occurred then or a very long time in the future because my rather insecure and stubborn nature would have convinced me that it was never the right time anyway. Endurance is a necessity in these cases, otherwise I know I would have certainly hung up my gloves. I had always been that way inclined.

I AM 13 YEARS old. I have 40 minutes to kill before I must return to the classroom. Everyone else has something to do during lunchtime break; they are either chatting amongst themselves in the canteen, or trotting around the corridors to visit friends and some of them are dotted around the school grounds, sitting out on the sun-drenched grass. I'm tired of sitting at my desk, pretending to do work that I have already finished during yesterday's lunch break. Instead, I sit in the toilet cubicle, still crying my eyes out and wishing I could be anywhere but here.

I rang Mum only moments ago, begging her to let me come home for the hour and telling her that I was miserable here. I wouldn't be able to stick this and was going to be unhappy for the next six years. I had heard the concern in her voice but she was still having none of it and told me to just try make it through another day and we would talk more about it when I got home. As I sit here sobbing, I hear chattering girls enter the room outside the cubicle door. Their laughing is high-pitched and gleeful. I stifle my crying as best I can, holding my breath until finally they leave. I break into uncontrollable whimpering once again.

It has been almost a month since I started secondary school. I am the only person from my primary school to come here and with the exception of one girl from my estate, I don't know anyone. Not that it matters all that much anyway because she is in a different class and we don't speak or even see each other. Lunchtimes are about an hour long and I never have anything to do during that time. Most days I do my homework or simply read what we have just finished or are about to learn in class. But I can only do that for so long because I never have any homework when I get home and am usually always ahead of the class now. Eating my lunch takes only five to ten minutes and every day, I end up in this cubicle crying and wishing I could go home again, where I feel safe and relieved.

I know it's breaking Mum's heart to have me calling her every day in such a state but I just have to. If for no other reason than to just have someone to talk to. I breathe in as deeply as I can, tidying myself up and wiping my tears. I think I must have a naturally sad face because whenever I walk past the main area of the school towards my classroom, a teacher always seems to stop me in my tracks to ask me if I'm okay, I wish they would just leave me alone. There's nothing they can do to help anyway so asking me such things is pointless.

Safely back in my seat, I open up our English textbook, put my head down and hope nobody will notice me or approach me. English is my favourite subject and as my eyes scan over and over a Seamus Heaney poem, I find some degree of ease in being here in this moment.

During class time, I usually feel fine because nobody is allowed to talk and when the teacher asks me a question, I always know the answer. This is because I spend every lunch time studying. Once during a religion class, however, we were asked to assign everyone a descriptive name beginning with the same letter as our own name. If your name was Sarah, your descriptive name would be *Super* Sarah and so on. As the teacher went through all the students, the class would shout out ideas until the right one was found. When it came to me, I was nervous and didn't say a word. Someone eventually yelled out 'Lonely Leanne!' and a few people laughed. The teacher refused the suggestion and was quick to pick some other adjective, but I don't remember what it is now. All I can think about is how I am *Lonely* Leanne.

As I glance over my notes on the Heaney poem, a girl shouts across the classroom, 'Hey you!' I don't realise it's directed at me so she yells even louder next time adding, 'Hey, *lonely* Leanne!' I look up to meet her gaze and see she's sitting with all the loudest girls in our class. She doesn't call me over but continues to shout from her spot against the wall.

'Who do you hang around with?' she asks. Straight away, I'm alarmed.

'Ehm', I choke, hoping my soft-spoken voice will carry across the room and various groups of girls. 'I'm the only person from my old school here so I don't know anybody.'

'No!' she laughs. 'Who do you hang out with outside of school?'

The truth is, I don't have any friends outside of school either.

Almost immediately after primary school, I never saw those girls again and for that summer at least, I was happy with not having any friends because to me, friends brought a whole world of trouble that I was just happier without. But I couldn't tell her or any of the other loud girls that. If I did, they would think I was weird and I would have no chance of making friends for the next six years. Instead, I list off a few random names, hoping this will satisfy her and that she will leave me alone. It doesn't and she continues to grin broadly, with the others giggling under their breath.

'Oh yeah, I know all them!' she chuckles. 'They live in Fassaroe, don't they?'

'Ehm, no.' I lie. 'They don't live in Bray at all. You wouldn't know them.'

'I might. What are their last names? I bet I'll know them.'

'I don't know any of their surnames' I tell her. This sends the whole group off into an outburst of giggles amongst themselves. A few other groups of girls have been listening as well and are looking at me with blank expressions – probably pity – trying to see my reaction.

'So then,' comes her voice once more, 'you really are *lonely* Leanne aren't you?'

I don't respond and this marks the end of my first conversation with another student. I heard one of the loud girls say through stifled laughter, 'Ah, you're so mean sometimes.' But they all continue in their hysteria nonetheless. Last week, Mum phoned the school to tell them that I was finding it difficult to make friends. Ms Dempsey, the deputy principle and renowned martyr of the school, took me around the grounds to better acquaint me with the place and show me all the things I could do to make friends and feel more at home. She was bright and friendly, and was like a grandmother figure for the entire school. But it was no good and after today, I don't think I want to be friends with anybody anyway. I just want to be left alone and do my time.

I think about my old primary school and how horrible those girls made it for me. But then, deep down inside, I wish I could go back. It doesn't matter how terrible those girls made my life back then because at least I was used to it. I've heard my Dad say before, 'Better the devil you know than the devil you don't' and now, I think I finally understand it. There is nothing familiar about this new school and sometimes I would rather be back in my old hell than stay in this new one for the next six years. I go back to the cubicle to cry. I stay there until the bell finally rings for class.

Maintaining a sense of familiarity in the things we do provides us with the security that we convince ourselves of, even if it's just a mere fabrication. In some of the most horrific circumstances, a person can often choose to endure rather than accept change purely because it's what they know best. I would go on to enjoy my years in secondary school immensely and always remember them fondly. Indeed, I still maintain that they were the best years of my life to date. But I resisted that transition just as I resisted the transition into recovery in the first weeks of therapy. In both cases, it would not take long before I finally submitted to the changes at hand, embraced them and then remembered each as the best thing I could have ever done at the time.

Two months into cognitive behavioural therapy with Michelle and I had taken the sessions into the bosom of my world, in much the same way as I had done with secondary school. In truth, she and I discussed my eating and purging habits very little. Naturally, it would crop up from meeting to meeting. When it did, I informed her, most honestly, how many times I had purged that week and how long a given fast had been. I think my honesty in that safe space surprised us both. I was shocked at how much I genuinely wanted to talk about this stuff. For all my secrecy surrounding such matters, once the floodgates had been opened, I poured it all out recklessly and unrestrictedly. It was terrifying and liberating at the same time.

The purpose of expressing the unvarnished truth about these habits was to enable Michelle and I to discover the 'triggers' that caused them. A trigger was something that compromised the control I had built my life around. In order to regain control, I would fast and purge, desperately attempting to empower myself as I saw fit. My triggers could be almost anything in the world and ranged extraordinarily both in scope and degree of importance.

The best example I can give in this case was an incident in

which I disclosed some personal information to an acquaintance. The information was trivial and of no importance. Nevertheless, when I observed that same person sharing all my secrets with a third party, I felt so wounded, that I reacted most destructively. It was as if in doing this, the person in whom I had placed trust, denied me of my right to privacy. The information, regardless of its significance, was mine to disclose or keep secret. In breaking my confidence, the decision had been taken away from me and thus, the control had been lost. This one, very minor incident resulted in a three day fast that was later followed by an almighty binge and two days of on-off purging.

In this way, the purpose of therapy was to encourage a sense of enlightenment and understanding about the things I did and why I did them. Understanding my actions was my most powerful weapon against them. In order to do this, however, I was required to analyse myself in such a way that would leave no rock unturned and no crevice unchartered. My past and who I was within it proved to be an integral part of this process. The more Michelle dug away at my thoughts and memories, the more I too was encouraged to pick up that psychological shovel and upturn the very foundations of my own mental architecture. I found myself reading old diaries that stretched back up to ten years in some cases. Michelle, of course, encouraged this; mostly because recovery requires the active participation of both the given psychologist and patient alike. It's not the same as merely taking a pill and hoping for the best; you have to want it and more importantly, work for it.

Reading my own words was the easiest way for me to fully

comprehend what had caused the mentality I then worked under. In relation to my recovery, the most interesting of all these diary entries were the ones from most recent years. I didn't need to interpret very much to know that from the age of about 17, a most distinct mentality had evolved. The shift was all too obvious, even to me and on those scribbled pages, I saw things that bothered me more than I ever remembered feeling.

Among other things, there had been clear signs of total confusion. Restarting a diet or a fast was an ongoing plot line, while undermining myself and focusing on my personal failures in doing these things were reoccurring themes throughout entries. I could also see how the minor daily occurrences in my life seemed to take on gargantuan weight over both my habits and thoughts. Everything I felt, thought and did was in reaction to these small transactions. My behaviours were reflections of everything that happened from day to day.

20th July 2009

How I feel about myself: 2/10

How I feel about my life: 3/10

I ate!! I was going to not eat and allow my body to slip back into ketosis. Only that way can I lose all this weight! The plan was to get down to around nine and a half stone by Friday, when I'll see my ex-boyfriend and all my friends. I'm currently about ten stone and definitely won't make that in three days! I'm so angry with myself. It was all going to be fine. Ami wanted to have tea together in her house before everyone got together for the evening. So I decided that I would have to eat otherwise they would notice. Once this was established, I fucked it all and allowed myself to binge beforehand ... We didn't even fucking eat!!! It was pointless. I had a good plan and was in a good place to actually do it properly and I fucked it down the drain for no reason, as usual. I'm so upset with myself. We're going drinking tomorrow night and now I don't know whether or not to have a drink. I wasn't going to because tomorrow was going to be day four of my fast. But now I don't know. I could avoid drinking and start over – see how far I get. Or if I do drink, I'll have to eat so as not to end up in pieces and in choosing this route, that means I may as well eat and drink until I see everyone on Friday. I'm so angry. Fat, stupid bitch!! I hate myself sometimes. I hate the way I look. I hate how stupid I am. I hate how lazy I am – lazy, selfish, ugly, liar – I hate it all and it's all me. It's my own fault I'm in this position. I just want to lose weight. I just want to go back to being nine stone again. Why the FUCK did I have to let it all pile back on? What is wrong with me? I hate myself. And sometimes, yes, in fact I would rather die than deal with this. Sometimes I really do just want to die.

Yours, Leanne

THE ISSUES SURROUNDING MY relationship with the opposite sex has always been a complicated one. Someone once said to me that they couldn't bring themselves to believe I really had that much trouble when it came to men and relationships.

'You're quite a pretty girl.' they had told me. 'There's no way a girl like yourself could have *that* much trouble.'

But in my early teen years, I experienced such a degree of rejection from men that the feeling solidified in my mind, thus hindering my ability to believe anything more of myself than being the lowest germ of the earth's surface. It never mattered how I 'blossomed', as I was very often informed of, because my mind interpreted what I was through this early rejection. Michelle once referred to it light-heartedly as an 'ugly duckling syndrome', whereby no matter how much I improved on the surface, I could never overcome that internal feeling that I was unattractive and more than this, utterly redundant. I felt unwanted and it was never more obvious than in my dealings with men. I adapted a rather nasty habit of validating myself through their advances and through their level of commitment to me. How committed they were to me measured my worth as a person. Moreover, it was this "ugly duckling syndrome" that time and time again inhibited my own ability to make a candid decision. Looking over those diaries, I realised that my friends had been right when they told me that my disease was greatly impacting my choices in men. And as someone with an apparent penchant for self-destruction, I wouldn't get away from the repercussions of these bad choices lightly.

18th March 2010

How I feel about myself: 0/10

How I feel about my life: 3/10

It's 3.00 am and all I want to do is crawl into a black hole and disappear. He hasn't talked to me in days now – and THAT was only because I rang him; a move that apparently freaked him out about us. Or at least that's the only logical conclusion I can come to. If we're speaking 'illogically', of course, I can come up with some different theories. Think of all the men and boys I've dated before – in the end, none of them wanted me. Now we can add him to that list.

I really thought he was different. He gave me hope that there was something left to love in me. People (namely the girls) will argue that it's not me and that, as always, 'it's him'. But let's be totally honest here – I am the common denominator of all these failures. I feel unlovable – I clearly am unlovable – they can never even stick around long enough to even see any potential to love me. He wanted a rather quick fling on the beach and nothing more. Surely, I'm not worthy of anything meaningful or important to them in their apparently prestigious lives.

Given my Dad's poor health this week, I was convinced he would get in touch – AND given that the two times we've been in contact was a result of my own initiation. I waited online for him; to present another opportunity to speak to him. But once again tonight, he declined the opportunity and went offline shortly after my own appearance. I feel sick. I don't feel an overwhelming sensation of pain. Instead I feel a sickening emptiness. I feel like a hole has been punched through me and left me completely hollow. I feel empty and worthless. I knew it wouldn't take long; no matter how wonderful he seemed, I knew that this high was only temporary – just a fleeting pleasure that would evaporate as fast as it had appeared.

I never know what I do wrong. In my own, apparently distorted head, things were going so well. He's going to finish it now, the next time we speak that is. That's what they do. They ignore you for as long as you let it drag on – until you finally accept the reality and ask them why they've ignored you for so long. Then they say that they're not ready for a relationship – just want to be 'alone' for a while, or are scared of getting into a relationship and are not 'ready for that kind of commitment' – it's all the same. And it's all bullshit. The real reason is looking them in the face as they diplomatically state their case. The real reason is me. I feel so sick. I hate myself sometimes. And often just wish I could be a completely different person. Maybe then I would be worth loving, God forbid even committing to. Until then though, I have to endure being the fat, worthless and insignificant little girl I am.

I can't take another failure. I am a failure. I can already feel my heart breaking. I don't think I ever even fully healed from the last few times – the incision is just getting deeper, and more infected. I am infected and damaged, and now worthless. I wish I could say that I'll lose all this weight, fix my skin and look irresistible the next time he sees me. But that won't happen; I've lost my ability to do it. I can't fast three days now without breaking it. I'm over ten and a half stone now again – and I wonder why they don't want me ... wake up girl.

Yours, Leanne

14th December 2009

How I feel about myself: 3/10

How I feel about my life: 5/10

Okay, I had planned on restarting this journal on a very positive note but unfortunately, that's not going to happen today. However, perhaps it's better that I begin again from the ground up. Because the ground is certainly where I feel and in such circumstances perhaps things can only get better.

I don't want to have an eating disorder. Whether or not I definitely have one I can't be sure but sometimes it certainly feels like it. Today, I feel fat and unattractive. I started trying to eat healthily yesterday but surprise, surprise; I have already failed. Mum and Dad ordered in some takeaway food tonight. I didn't want it but I just couldn't bring myself to say no. How weak is that? This is why I sometimes don't feel entirely normal. A normal person could have at least SOME self control and say a simple 'No, thank you.' But not me? Well that's me all over; reckless and generally incredibly weak.

I didn't really feel this way on Saturday night. While in the midst of trying to get over the last break-up, I went down to the pub with all the girls. It was good fun and I felt sexy because I was hit on by several guys. Yes, yes, I know what you're thinking – she's just using male attention to validate herself! Well that being acknowledged, can we just continue with the business of talking? Sometimes it's like trying to get my fix. If I feel really low, I just have to go down to the strip and I'll be full to the brim with compliments and they'll do until the next time it all starts to turn bad again. Is that really pathetic? What am I saying, yes of course it is. Get over yourself Leanne, you know nobody really means any of those compliments they give you.

I went to the gym yesterday and again today. I'm proud that I dragged my lazy ass even over there but if I'm being honest, I don't feel *like whatever I'm doing is going to have any noticeable results. I don't know if I'm even physically able to do any more exercise, but it's like it's just not going to change anything because maybe I'm not doing it right or something. Pessimistic, I know, but I've promised myself that no matter what I think, I'm going to go over there every day regardless. However, this being said, I still don't feel particularly good about myself. I'm the heaviest I've been in a VERY long time now and generally just feel like a hippo. I'd give anything to lose weight. I tried the healthy eating gig and it just wasn't working, or at least not fast enough. I'll just have to stop eating altogether again. Doing that is the only thing that makes a difference and the only thing that makes me feel good. Moreover, I made myself sick again tonight after the takeaway. I haven't done that in two days now and I feel totally ashamed. Firstly, because I wish I hadn't eaten that disgusting meal (things were going so well beforehand) and secondly, because purging is the most undignified thing a person can do and stands only to highlight both my lack of willpower and utter weakness of character. The only reason how I feel about myself is rated at three and not at zero today is purely because of the attention everyone gave me on Saturday. Without that, I would definitely have been feeling much worse. Tomorrow will be better. I've promised myself this. I'll work out in the morning, study in the afternoon and go to the gym in the evening – while not letting myself go above 200 calories.*

Actually, that brings me to why I have rated 'how I feel about my life' as so low today. I really should study. And to be honest, I'm using this diary entry as a form of procrastination. It's too late now. It's 10.00 pm and when I finish this I just want to sleep. I don't have the energy for anything else. But I can't deny anymore that I am doing poorly in college to say the least. I've sacrificed some subjects for others, meaning that while I'm coming out with A's and B's in certain modules, I'm actually failing others completely. Even at that, I know those grades aren't going to last because I can feel myself slipping away. And if I can't even keep myself together, there's no way in hell I can keep it all together for college. I'm not sure what this means for second year, nor how I'm going to explain things to my parents. If I can keep this from them totally, I will. My supposed 'intelligence' is sometimes all I have going for me. I can't bear the thought of people doubting it. Excelling in academia is often all that I am. I'm not willing to allow people to think otherwise.

I desperately hope tomorrow is better. I hate feeling like such a failure.

Yours, Leanne

2ⁿᵈ July 2009

How I feel about myself: 1/10

How I feel about my life: 2/10

So, I finally talked to him. It was a result of my initiation, of course. He seemed as distant as he always is with me and did everything but laugh outright in my face. So what does that mean? It means I'm an idiot for continuing this. I don't know what's wrong with me. Everything feels like it's slipping out of my control and though I know he doesn't help that feeling, I just can't bear to let him slip as well. It'll just be another failure.

Same old Leanne; I just can't find the strength for this. I know this to be true and yet, I feel calm since talking to him. I've been so wound up, screwed so tight and on the brink of absolute meltdown. But since talking to him I feel relaxed again – like I've gotten a much needed fix. I know it's of no importance in the greater scheme of things but men are like a drug to me; especially when I feel very attached, as I do now. I'm calm for now and that brief discussion with him should tide me over for a while.

I'm not so sad as to be unaware of when a guy has lost interest. I've plenty of experience in the 'getting-indirectly-dumped field.' Signs when a guy has lost interest: Firstly, he stops getting in touch – this is not to say you stop communicating. But let's be honest: when you're the desperate bitch always having to text and/or strike up a conversation first, it's probably not a good sign. Secondly, on the now rare occasions that you do speak – as a result of your initiation of course – he's short answers and not a lot of talk. For example you text saying, 'Hey how have you been? Any news?' and the reply you get is, 'Good. You?' And to this I think it also apt to add that if these conversations are via online chat, it's worth taking into consideration how long you're waiting for a reply. Feels like too long? It probably is – meaning he has more important conversations to be having. So get over it. Thirdly, since WHEN do girls have to organise to meet up? Need I say more. And finally, he's not making ANY commitment!! Let me guess – he's just scared about getting into a relationship? Ha, you wish it was that simple to fix. Let me clear it up for you; it's not him, it's you. Sort yourself out and maybe you will be worth the commitment you want so desperately. Pathetic.

I'm going to start dieting tomorrow and I'm determined to make it work. They call this a disease. If that's the case, I will make my disease my best friend. My 'illness' will make me everything I need to be to continue in the pursuit of perfection. I'm so sick of looking at skinny girls and wishing I had their bodies. I will be skinny and beautiful beyond recognition. Then no one will ever again be able to refuse me or deny anything. I will make myself an indispensable gem to the world and everyone in it. I just need to be logical about this and make a plan. Fix my skin, which has been giving me hassle lately. Sort out my weight. Everything else will fall into place. I can do this. I did it before. I'll do it again. I just have to get past my own lethargy and laziness; THAT is my biggest obstacle. I need to get a job, get a new car, become skinny, lose the spots, and finally make myself irresistible to the society I hate so much. I can do this. Please Christ, help me before I kill myself.

Yours, Leanne

THE IMPORTANCE I ONCE placed on the superficial validation of men, shocks me to this day. To a large extent, I'm still ashamed of these diary entries because they highlight the lowest and most embarrassing parts of who I used to be. But in fully understanding myself and the mentality that enabled my bulimia, they are a necessity and stand as proof in my own mind of just how low one individual can sink.

There has never been any blame in the development of my illness or at least not in my own head anyway. I have never recalled a person, circumstance or singular reason as to why I became so sick.

But the factors that contributed to my illness stretched far and wide and tapped into every aspect of the life of any contemporary teenager. Western culture I believe has a great deal to do with this, as it has not only shaped civilisation as we know it, but continues to demand ongoing change from the society by which it is inhabited. As this western culture grows through its own evolution, it alters and contorts that same evolution of the individual. The influence of the media on me throughout my disease was something that I could not ignore upon reflection. Is this to say that the media alone was responsible for my bulimia? No, clearly not. I think we've come far enough in our discussion now to know that this isn't the case. But to attribute nothing at all to the hierarchal industries that define contemporary beauty, would also be a gross lie.

18th November 2007

How I feel about myself: 1/10

How I feel about my life: 7/10

Woke up this morning and quite simply wanted to die. I felt like the most revolting person on the planet. From my horribly spotty face to the piles of fat that cling to and consume my whole body, I felt like I would be prettier in death than as I am right now. Surely no woman is meant to look like this. If what magazines tell me is true, surely I am behind the human race in evolution. I am the genetic garbage of mankind. But no more. I can make myself worthy of more than this if I try and I have the discipline to show it. I love school but perhaps I need to put it on the back burner for a while, as there are more important things to be dealt with now. As such, I have allocated a few weeks to be selfish and think about nothing but myself.

Do other girls think this way? Perhaps. But with a bit of luck, telling myself these truths will eventually help me shed the necessary weight so that once it's finally gone, I can adopt a healthy lifestyle from then on. I am currently about twelve and a half stone. The goal is to get down to nine stone before starting college next year. This is possible. And I will do anything. My friends need not know. I'll tell them about it when I've lost the weight and when I'm in the process of 'living healthily.' If losing weight is unhealthy well then by God, I must make myself the most unhealthy girl in all of Ireland.

I'll be carrying this out by doing several things. Firstly, I have gym membership and I WILL use it every day and moreover, I will exercise even more at home until I feel it's finally making a difference. If I could become addicted to exercise, I think things in my life would become simpler. But that's not going to happen so for now, I will bully myself into enjoying the pain of extensive workouts. I will be following a STRICT low-calorie diet. I'm allowing myself about 500 calories a day. On a rough basis, this will consist of: an apple and coffee for breakfast; three rice cakes for lunch; and finally, chicken and lettuce for dinner. I am to drink two litres of water a day and will hopefully remember to take the necessary vitamin tablets at each meal. This will hopefully be enough to transform me from this horrible creature I've turned into something that can just mildly resemble the women I see all the time now.

I also heard of what's called the Maple Syrup Detox Diet. Apparently, loads of celebrities use it to shed pounds fast. I've heard of some celebrities dropping around 20lbs within a fortnight while on it. I like the sound of it because it's a lot of weight loss and very little time. I don't have time to lose weight the normal way because I feel like a ticking time bomb. Not to mention the fact that I just can't stand being this size anymore. I have to fix this NOW. I eat nothing for about ten days and instead, drink this concoction of water, maple syrup and cayenne pepper. If I can get enough breathing room, I'll try it for as long as I can.

My main problem at the moment is being given the space to carry out any diet at all. Aside from the girls now breathing down my neck because once or twice they noticed me skipping my lunch at break time, my mum – in a totally counterproductive way – has been on my back and I think would notice my attempts to carry out any of the above. I just need to dodge her suspicions as much as possible. I can just lie to the girls, but my mum will be more aware, as she lives with me. But it is manageable. A growing obsession with the gym will be encouraged, as she's all for it. So that's one thing down. The diet will be slightly trickier. She works most days or is out of the house, so I'm sure I could have breakfast and lunch covered. It's just dinner. But perhaps if I just lie to her about what I've already eaten that day, she might just go along with what I want for dinner.

Hopefully, tomorrow I'll feel better about myself because I'll have *started the weight loss plan. My potential is my biggest weapon and one of the reasons for how I've rated my feeling on life today. Moreover, I rethought my life. And though I am disgusted with how fat I have allowed myself to become, my life is good. And I know that with some discipline and control, I will match how I look to how good I could look in time and how great it could be. All those celebrities, models, actresses – there's no way they look that way without a little discipline. If they can do it, so can I. I'm only 17 but one day, I will be more famous than all of them combined and I will be damn sure to look the part.*

I'm going out tonight using Natalie's I.D. So once I've had time to get over the trauma of finding something slimming to wear, I plan on simply drinking myself into one final oblivion, in celebration of what is to come. I will do this. I know I can.

Yours, Leanne.

I SUPPOSE IT'S A very unfair to claim that any individual in the media is encouraging eating disorders among young girls today. I'm not making that claim anyway. If anything, I think I have a great deal of pity for such public figures. Allow me to explain; you see, as a victim of such effects, I do contend that some responsibility is to be attributed to particular media industries today. The people and organisations who define what beauty is in the modern world seem dead set on alleviating themselves of any implication in such things. But the reality is that when their work influences modern living as it does, they cannot surely escape that involvement. Sure, they may claim it to be art. And yet, art stops being so exclusively when it becomes a dictation as to how people choose to live their lives – albeit healthily or in my case, very unhealthily indeed. Such 'art' relies on this societal involvement to fuel its progression in the first place. And while I of all people hold out hope for major changes to take place within these realms that so easily influence daily living, my pessimism leaves me to doubt as much.

As regards the familiar faces that are splashed across weekly magazines and television programmes, I view them not as propagators in this vicious cause, but as victims. The emaciation we see in photographs, which is usually glorified is a result of this monstrous 'beauty machine' that has gripped western culture. The ideal of what beauty is has always been there, yes, but I don't think it has ever before been at such a crucial point, whereby women such as myself are starving themselves to embody it. Surely the human race has come too far to remain so painfully naive.

It's all very easy to say these things now, of course. After taking my body and mind to some of the darkest places a person can go, one can't but help retain a degree of anger perhaps even resentment, to the exterior influences that guided me down that pathway. But then again, I've had the very good fortune of therapy and recovery to solidify these opinions and perhaps even make them stubborn. At the time, I never perceived the media this way. The question in my mind at that time was not whether or not it was the right direction, but simply whether or not I could keep up to speed with it. As it turned out, I couldn't. I realised this again and again throughout my bulimia and every moment of clarification served to fragment me even further. It hurts me still to know that for so long, I endured suicidal thoughts for the sake of 'looking good enough'.

25th September 2009

How I feel about myself: 0/10

How I feel about my life: 0/10

This is impossible. It feels like life is killing me. And worst of all, I can't blame this feeling on very unfortunate circumstances or on things that are out of my control; this feeling is a result of my own failings. Sure, I can say – and have been doing so for a long time – that I feel fucked in life because I have an 'eating disorder.' Is this the reason I feel like such a failure? No. I am a failure because I can't – no, I choose – not to do anything better with myself.

I'm just sick of being bad at everything I try. No matter what I do, I seem to do it wrong. It kills me thinking back to a time when I felt I could do anything; when I felt I was good at so many things. I was a good student, got amazing grades, didn't cause my parents so much stress, didn't cost them so much money, could write and write and never tire of it, could draw anything in the world and make it almost photographic, could have any guy I wanted and still not give a shit. Now, I feel like a failure who has been making excuses for herself so as to avoid what needs to be done.

And what needs to be done is more than I think I can handle. I now feel that this is impossible.

I want to kill myself. I held a scissors to my arm and pressed down. But I couldn't go through with it – I was too afraid of the pain. I can't stand this any longer. I can't live with an eating disorder anymore but at the same time, I can't bring myself to live as everyone else does. Everyone is going to think I'm a big, fat failure. I want to die. I want to go into a hole and never come out. I hate myself. I am a monster. I'm a failure and I am unlovable. He is becoming more and more distant. He doesn't want me – nobody does. I am problematic, ugly and unlovable. I want to die. I want someone to kill me. I hate myself. I hate what I am. I just want to give up. I'm nothing more than a problem to the people I love most. I don't want to be their problem anymore. Please God, save me. And if you can't, please just kill me.

Yours, Leanne.

YOU WOULD PROBABLY ASSUME that looking back on all these vicious words hurts me very badly. During recovery, they didn't. I was never in denial about how I'd once felt on so many things. Besides, by that point, I was no longer reading them merely to dwell on the horrible feelings they came with; I was reading them so I could see myself fully, all the good and all the bad rolled into one. Both were required to attain any level of understanding about myself and my disease.

I embraced therapy to the best of my ability. If not for the sake of getting better, but also because it just made me feel better at that time. I still had doubts about whether or not it was what I truly wanted and for a while, was convinced that all it would result in was being physically larger in weight. Others around me – my family included, as they now knew about my weekly attendance – passed comments often on how I appeared brighter, more like the person they'd known before. I was happy to please them, as it was something I hadn't been able to do in so very long. At the same time, however, some days it felt like I had been reverted back to my childhood and like I had to stay in line with all the 'grown-ups' around me, as they watched me play in the sand. It's ironic how one seeks out a sense of control in such a horrific way and while you think you're gaining more and more, the reality is that you are stamping a guarantee that you may lose that control forever.

Recovery in general was an up and down battle. Some days I wanted it so badly, while on other days I neither cared for it nor wanted it. And on occasion, I went as far as to believe that everyone around me was utterly against me. I convinced myself that they had no interest or care for what I wanted anymore; that the only interest they took in me was always related to what they believed I 'needed.' Throughout my therapy I seemed to be entirely dependent on others; my family, my friends and Michelle herself. It felt to a large extent like I had surrendered something of great proportions, like I had handed myself over to a more powerful force. I wondered sometimes if these people would still be around once they had 'fixed' me. This was a dangerous thought and threatened the development of my recovery because it fuelled the idea that once finished and once 'fixed', I would have nothing left. I would have nothing left of myself or of the people around me. This was the risk I thought I'd taken and it wounded me deeply.

Changing my eating habits became a little easier, although stopping them was still a struggle in itself. It's just not that simple. You don't flip a switch and undo all that you've been taught for so long. As I grew to understand my actions more and how my subconscious ways of thinking dictated to those actions, I found myself thinking on the surface level when it came to food.

In this way, I certainly saw improvements in my eating. I avoided fasts as much as I could, attempting to replace them with healthy eating. But the purging was very difficult to break. The phrase, 'it's a daily battle' is an understatement in this case. It's an hourly battle, every minute was a challenge for me. For other people, eating is just a natural part of their day. It fuels their day. But for a bulimic, eating and the consequences of eating are what your day revolves around. Every meal is agonized over, trying to consume it and hold it down thereafter. Equally, the time spent not eating is usually spent obsessing or worrying about the next time you have to eat and what will happen to your body when you do. Each meal is more weight and getting past this notion was incredibly problematic for me. Time and endurance were the only healers as it turned out and to this day, I still struggle.

Getting help for an eating disorder is naturally one of the

hardest things a person must do. For the most part, this is because before you may go down this route, you must first accept that there is in fact something wrong with you. I never wanted anything to be wrong with me. I never wanted to be sick. On the contrary, I had built an entire fabrication around myself that I was a hard-working, would-be successful girl who generally maintained a bright-eyed and bushy-tailed demeanour. To admit the truth was to contradict this facade, which I wasn't ready to do for a very long time. Even harder than admitting the lie to yourself, is doing so with the people around you. It would be at least a year and a half into my illness before I ever made the admission to friends and family that I was sick and that I had been suffering bulimia nervosa.

Once I had accepted and more importantly, admitted, that I had a problem, the changes I saw in myself were of monumental proportions. Be that as it may, opening those doors is like opening a can of worms. This is true in particular cases, such as my own, when you choose to share your story with others so earnestly. There remains now, as there was even at that time, a paralysing fear. It is part of the reason I kept my secret life with bulimia hidden for so long and a fear that embodies everything that is wrong with the common mentality surrounding eating disorders. I was afraid then – as I have been from time to time since beginning this story – that people would not *believe* me.

It was the one factor that ensured I would keep my hidden

'friend' shut away from the rest of the world both during my illness. Why this fear remains so powerful relates back to the matter of denial, which I believe many if not all bulimics and anorexics alike, experience at some point while sick; usually at the beginning I would imagine, but that's not to say it can't last years and maybe until it's too late. To explain it better, I may begin by saying that I spent so long in denial about my mental illness that acknowledging the problem was arguably the biggest hurdle towards recovery. Not fully trusting the notion, it took months of tears and heartache on both my part and that of my loved ones, to finally solidify this to be fact. Consequently, the possibility of others not believing me was what kept me caged for so long. Disbelief would surely threaten everything I had worked towards as it would compromise my own fight against denial and my own faith in that what my friends and family were telling me was true. I was bulimic. But if others could not accept this, I wasn't sure if I had any chance of fully committing to the idea myself.

I broached this issue once with Michelle. I had been struggling at university since I first began in September of 2009. Mid-way though my second semester of that first academic year, I thought I would drop out. With high fees to pay and my families low finances, I knew that my bulimia had cost me my education. Financially speaking, I could never remedy the damage that had been done.

As fortune and apparently sympathetic souls would have it, the college offered an extenuating circumstances route that students could avail of in the case of bereavement, illness and so on. All that was needed was a letter of clarification from both my doctor and my psychologist. This was not a problem, as Michelle had been treating me for several months by then and my doctor had given the referral, as well as a prescription for Xanax to help curb my out-of-control anxiety. So, I was granted extenuating circumstances due to illness. It didn't remedy all finances but certainly made my continuation in university possible at least.

Alas, I met the entire ordeal with a level of dissatisfaction. When Michelle and I addressed the matter she asked very directly, 'What's the problem, Leanne?'

'What if I'm not really that sick?' I asked in reply.

'What do you mean?'

'I mean, I have you and all these people in college now thinking I'm really sick with anxiety, an eating disorder and God knows what else. But what if you're all wrong? Maybe I've just convinced you all of something that isn't really there.'

At these words, she smiled broadly and seemed to almost fight a laugh while saying, 'Is that what you really think?'

I nodded certainly.

'Leanne,' she started. 'I hate to break it to you but you're not *that* smart.'

'What?'

'Do you really think you're so smart that you can fool me and all those administrators in your university? I hate to break it to you but you're not. I didn't go through years of studying psychology to get the qualifications I have – and neither did those people – to be easily *tricked* by any girl who walks in and claims to have an eating disorder. You wouldn't do that anyway, I *know* you wouldn't. But what concerns me more, Leanne, do you really think you're *that* deceptive? I mean, do you really think you're so manipulative that you could lie all this time about being unwell when you're really not?'

It was a lot to take in. As she spoke about herself and the other professionals, whom I'd convinced myself that I had 'fooled', I laughed along, feeling rather foolish. But it was the latter part of her statement that stopped me dead in my tracks. In all honesty, yes, I did think I was manipulative enough to do it. If only she knew how monstrous I thought I was. Perhaps she did but just hadn't brought it up yet.

'Sometimes,' I replied in answer to her question. She looked a little stunned and perhaps a bit disappointed.

'Well,' she gasped, 'maybe *that* is something we need to look a bit closer at then.'

I underwent about six months of cognitive behavioural therapy with Michelle. During that time, we had explored the bullying I suffered as a child and how I had carried those painful messages on into my teenage years, digesting them and thus coming out with a warped view of myself and my place in the world. We talked about my relationships with the members of my family and on one occasion, even brought my mother in to discuss these relationships and all their flaws. We talked about my body image and how I had placed so much value on something that was distorted anyway; it was never going to be a winning situation this way. We talked about men and the issue of self-worth, how I qualified myself as worthy both to them and everyone else. We talked about my eating habits, why I carried out the behaviours I did and how I interpreted them as the only means of empowerment and the gaining of control. The list was endless and it took me to places within myself I never knew existed. Or if I did, I had long forgotten about them.

Therapy had not been what I expected it to be; in truth, it was more positive than I could have ever hoped for. What it did for me was to provide the tools that would strengthen me as I went on to rebuild a lost life. When Michelle and I were in agreement that I was ready to retake the reigns of control over my life, my emotions and my mental health, it was an oddly sad goodbye. Armed with the power of knowledge, enlightenment, understanding and a new sense of resolution, I left that office in a state of transformation. Recovery does not finish with therapy; quite the contrary in fact. Recovery begins with professional help – or at least it did for me – and is continued through the determination and unyielding hope of the individual.

Things were not perfect the day I finished my sessions with Michelle and I would continue to struggle with the temptations of fasting and purging for a long time thereafter. But if nothing else, I left that day with a renewed hope; not in people, or the world, or God, or success, or even *her*. I left with a strange faith in myself. And it was all I needed for the time being.

27th June 2010

How I feel about myself: 7/10

How I feel about my life: 8/10

My apologies for not writing recently; I've been swamped making last-minute preparations for my trip to India. I think it's going to do me the world of good spending a month in a place like Delhi. I need to get away from this life that has so often been a cage to me.

I finished therapy with Michelle recently and though I have mixed feelings about having to cope without her, I've discovered one thing to be absolutely certain: the kindness of others will never fail to astound me. Despite what we may think, people love other people. It's in our nature to help and hope that, in turn, we'll receive help when needed. Moreover, people have the capacity to be more understanding than I think I've given them credit for. Having reached some of the worst conditions I have ever emotionally and physically experienced over this last year or two, I think I can safely say that ... well, everything's going to be okay. I was on fire. And now, I just have to sift through the ashes and wait for a change of wind to eventually blow them away. Where that's going to come from I can't be entirely sure. But for now, I reckon it will eventually come from me. All I have to do is take that responsibility.

Life is a funny thing. We claim it to be our own; but the truth is, it's not. It belongs to something much bigger. We, like everything else, are transient. This life is temporary and everything about us is temporary. What we call our life is nothing more than borrowed energy from something much bigger – nature, the universe, God – whatever floats your boat. And one day, when we pass, we will give that energy back to the world we borrowed it from in the first place.

I've come to the conclusion that I am in fact something very small – but that's okay; because I'm just a very small part of something much bigger. It's bigger than any of us can imagine. We're not running on our own time, nor our own energy – it's not ours to run on. And, I suppose, seeing as we're running on someone else's time, it's what we decide to do with this borrowed energy that really makes all the difference.

Ultimately, what people don't want to face is the reality of how utterly powerless we are. We can't stop this process – or control it. So we try to find other ways of claiming power; money, status, control over others or in my case, what I've put myself through for so long now and what I'm now sick to death of writing about. But that's not what makes us powerful beings. The human mind, though temporary, is so complex; so boggling that even science can't fully grasp it. Why? Because we're not scientifically advanced enough yet? Sometimes I don't think so. Maybe it's something much bigger than even science. And, in a sense, that's what makes us powerful. And the best – though I'm sure for some people the worst – thing about this kind of power is that it's something that can't be flaunted or even hindered. Well, not if you protect it.

My eating disorder didn't make me powerless to its effects. I did.

I didn't want the responsibility and in many ways, it's just easier to let someone else control you. The truth is that when you come to the realisation that no one is ever really in control, life becomes much easier. I'm not in control and neither is my eating disorder, something much bigger is. All I have to do is finally take responsibility – for this borrowed time I've been given, this transient existence. And I think I'm ready to do that. I'm ready to take responsibility for my own borrowed energy.

I don't know what's going to happen in the future and I know it's not going to be perfect. But for now, at least – finally – I can hope once more.

Yours as always, Leanne

REGENERATION

As stated at the beginning of this memoir, I have never liked the term bulimia. This is mostly because the phrase cannot fully encapsulate all that I have detailed here to you, dear reader. Such a small word surely cannot be sufficient. Quite simply, it's just not enough. Similarly, neither is the word 'recovery' because, it does not always have a definite beginning or end; not to mention how everything within those two bookends is a muddled haze of complexity. To be frank, bulimia – along with any eating disorder – does not end with recovery alone. Recovery in my own mind at least, is the time in which you heal those psychological wounds that were created by the disease itself. It involves catering to the emotional scars left behind and finding peace with the memories you can never forget or change.

Within recovery, I began a long and arduous process of regeneration. While recovery alone was the psychological reversal of all that she – the vicious creature that inhabited my brain – had brought me to believe, the process of regeneration saw me attempting to rebuild the life that I had sacrificed for her. Moreover, it was the process in which I sought to rebuild myself. It was as if I had been dead, as if I somehow had to resurrect myself from the ashes of my own destructiveness. My biggest fear with letting her go had always been that without her, there would be nothing left of me. And in truth, this was nearly the case. Nevertheless, I had to cling to that hope that there was still something there to save, something worth the life my bulimia had almost ruined.

It's extraordinarily difficult to know where to begin in reconstructing a lost life from the foundation levels up again. One of the first steps was to find reconciliation with my past and the painful memories that had kept me trapped for so many years. I agonized over those ancient diaries, remembering the bullies and the true extent of all the damage they had caused. There was one memory, that I dwelled on more than others in my pursuit of long overdue resolution with that past.

I AM TWELVE YEARS old. Primary school is coming to an end and while I'm scared of what's to come this September in a new school, I cannot wait for the summer to commence. It will be two months of torture-free bliss in which I can enjoy the freedom of comfort and security.

The girls in school were particularly bad this week. After one argument, none of them were talking to me anymore. I had nobody to talk to at lunchtime while the boys played desk football and in the end, I had to stay inside the school during yard time. That was why I had become a prefect. It was so I could escape their refusal to be my friend and maybe even pretend it wasn't happening.

I used to be best friends with one of the girls, but now she is one of those who weren't talking to me. We were the best artists in the class and could draw anything. She was also good at Gaelic football and I liked the way she wrote. It had been an instant connection. We can't be friends the way we used to be because then she will be excluded like me. I won't ask her to do that because no matter how bad I feel, I wouldn't like to think that I'm causing anyone else to feel this way too.

Today I came home crying because the girls have been telling lies about me and saying bad things. When Mum asks me what is wrong, I can't bring myself to fully explain because I don't want her knowing what the girls in school say about me. I don't want her to ever think those things about me and it's best that the idea is just never put in her head at all. I run into my bedroom, unable to watch as she too starts to cry. This upsets her just as much as it upsets me and it breaks my heart. As I heave and sob into my pillow on my bed, wishing there was something I could do to change everything and stop Mum from crying, I hear Mum talking in her usual, loud phone voice. Walking out of my bedroom and leaning over the banisters of the stairs, as I've done so many times on sleepless nights, I hear Mum yelling down the phone through broken tears.

'I just don't know what to do anymore,' she cries. 'It's gone too far and I just can't watch her go through this anymore.'

I assume that she has called my grandmother and is telling her how hard this is, hoping for somebody to throw her a maternal life-jacket. I return to my foetal position on the bed where I cry even harder because I am making Mum's life so hard on her. It goes quite downstairs, except for Mum's stifled sobbing into a seat cushion in the sitting room. I try to be as quiet as possible, tears still flowing down my cheeks. I don't want to make this any worse than it is and hearing me upset will surely make Mum worse. Within about ten minutes of hearing Mum on the telephone, the doorbell rings and I bolt back to my place atop the stairs. When the door opens, I can hear violent outburst of crying fill the hallway. Leaning over a little further, I watch as one of the girls from school and her mother pass the bottom of the stairs and make their way into the kitchen with Mum. I'm terrified of what is happening and start to shake from head to toe.

'Leanne,' Mum calls. 'Babe, come on down for a minute please.'

I burst into renewed and heavier tears, as if this is the first time I've ever cried in my life. When I reach the kitchen, all three of them are still standing. My friend's mother looks at me briefly through watered eyes and starts to weep uncontrollably. She can't look at me for very long and begins to address my mother again. Everyone is crying; my friend, her mother, my mum and me. There is a raw, red mark on my friend's arm where her mother clearly dragged her into the house with a tight grip. She and I do not look at each other, but both cry silently as we watch our mothers' exchange.

'I just *had* to call,' my mum bleats out, still red and puffy in the face. 'I just can't let this go on. If only you knew what it was doing to her.'

'No, no,' my friend's mother interrupts. 'I'm so glad you did. I'm absolutely mortified. I was only today giving a seminar about bullying in the workplace. I never had any idea my own daughter could be doing it in school. I'm so sorry. I'm just completely mortified.'

'She's not the ringleader, but we need to do what we can and I've just reached the end of my tether. I don't know what to do anymore.'

The two women are hysterical and grip one another in an awkward hug as they cry it out. My friend's head is bent right down to the ground, but I can still see how her forehead is crinkled with lines of worry and distress. I cry too. On top of everything, I now feel guilty that I have caused such chaos among everyone. If only I could have kept my mouth shut about it all and nobody would be as sad as they all are now.

'Leanne,' my mum whimpers as she wipes her face. 'Why don't you go upstairs and have a chat between the two of you.'

At these words, my body goes into shock and I am temporarily glued to the floor upon which I stand. I feel like I've been set on fire and my heart pounds in my chest so violently I think it will jump out of my throat. I don't look at my friend because I'm scared to. Instead, I start to make my way up the stairs and can hear her following behind me, as well as Mum fiddling with the kettle in the kitchen.

My friend and I sit face to face on my bed, both of us crying and obviously embarrassed by this whole situation. I try to take a deep breath but it feels like my airways have been disconnected. I try to prepare myself for what is about to come. My friend is going to give out to me. She's going to tell me that I'm really in for it now. What happens next is the biggest shock I have ever had since meeting those girls. My friend breaks down even further into tears, trying to catch her voice.

'I'm so *sorry*!' she blurts out, looking at me for the first time since she entered my house. I'm so taken aback that I don't say anything at all.

'I'm so sorry, Leanne! I really am. I didn't know what to do; you know what the girls are like. I was just scared because if they didn't do it to you, they could do it to me or whoever else. I know that's no good now but I really am sorry. We used to be best friends and now I've ruined it all. I didn't mean it and I didn't realise how bad it had gotten until today. I'm really sorry, please don't be mad at me. You're my best friend and I never meant to hurt you.'

With this she breaks down once more, cut off by her own heavy sobs. She buries her red face into her hands and bends forward, covering herself over entirely. I cry too and for a while, nobody says anything. Amidst all the tears, there's just no room for talking. When we both calm down slightly, she can't look at me again.

'It's okay.' I whisper.

'What?' she looks stunned and almost doubles back on herself.

'It's okay.' I say again, a little louder this time. This time she has heard me and once again, crumbles under her own crying and covers her face again. As I watch her deteriorate again in front of my eyes, a strange sensation starts to take over my body. The damp cloud that hung over me lifts ever so slightly. Not knowing what else to do I lean forward, wrap my arms around her and hug her as tight as I can. She grips my arms in return and together we cry for what feels like hours.

It feels like the longest cry of my life and the next time I look at her, I see the friend I thought I'd lost.

In an ideal world and a perfect story, this event would have been the turning point in the bullying. Although my friend never participated in the bullying again, whenever the girls were acting up or giving me a hard time, she merely abstained. Knowing her own fears now, was enough for me and I never held it against her. But the bullying continued right until the end of sixth class and I never saw the girls again after that time. The vulnerability with which my friend exposed herself that day touched a part of me so tender that to this day, I often wonder where she is in her life today and if she's happy. I hope she is.

I had forgiven her in an instant. I had seen all my fears and all my pain splashed across her tear stained face and I had forgiven her before she even asked it. Children are simple that way. It doesn't take much to bring out the best in them and the concept of 'forgive and forget' is never better exemplified than with a child. Doing just this as I've gotten older, however, has become gradually harder. The scars that my childhood bullying imprinted on me became old war wounds that were integral to the shaping of my character. For years, I carried them on my skin, terrified that at any moment they could burst wide open again and everything underneath would bleed out.

Not long before I started therapy, I had been walking along the seafront when I saw one of the girls who bullied me and some girl whom I did not know. She was within 20 yards of me. I remember how my body seized up at the sight of her and I got a lump in my throat that threatened to burst under the pressure of the moment. Walking by her, my eyes met hers for a rather prolonged moment. Taking me in, there was no trace of recognition in her eyes and they drifted away from me and on to the next passer-by. She didn't even recognise me, she had no idea who had just passed her so casually on the street. I recalled thereafter feeling a surging sense of anger ensue. I thought to myself, *How dare she not know me. How dare she not know the face she tortured so much and for so long.*

Michelle once described this as though I was walking around with more than just one person in me. On top of the teenager I had become, I held the hand of the little girl I was then. She had never left me and in everything I did or thought in later years, she was still there and we faced it all together. Her presence wasn't the problem; the problem was just that I hadn't been taking care of that little girl well enough. Moreover, I believe that it was around the time that I got sick that I let go of that little hand. I forgot all about her and abandoned her for the darkness within. She represented everything in my past I so desperately wanted to forget and for this, I was scared to have her in my life. There could have been only one remedy for all the pain. I had to forgive my past. Only in doing this could I truly discover the unblemished beauty of the person beneath it. We would do it together, that little girl and I. And I swore to her that I would never let go of her hand again. I would keep her with me always and protect her from all the bullies in the world.

I would not be alone in doing this or anything else for that matter. There came a point through this process of regeneration that I had to re-evaluate my relationship with God; or at least, what was left of it. In hindsight, God had never left my life but rather, I simply did not allow a place for Him within it. Throughout my illness, I'd had my doubts of what this 'God' idea truly entailed. More than anything that came before and even after this period of my life, nothing tested my faith quite so much as my bulimia. It called into question the certainty and enduring power of my own faith. For the most part, I think I then felt like God had abandoned me to my misery. Of course the reality was the complete opposite of this, which I learned in time, but being caught in the undertow of my own sick ocean lead me to find faith only in God's apparent indifference. I had many quarrels with Him and for a long time both during and after recovery, had to search deep within for any chance of reconnection with the spirituality that once guided me through life.

This involved dwelling – for months on end – on the purpose of God in my life, the true extent of my belief both in his presence and his power and finally, whether I felt ready to open up that line of connection once again. I began attending mass again; something that I had almost forgotten about entirely while being sick. The institution of Catholicism did not govern the internal flame I fought to keep burning, but it definitely helped. If not for the resurrection of my faith, then at least for that lost sense of spiritual community shared between so many people.

You may use the terminology of 'God' quite loosely here, as my idea of what the very word means has broadened greatly since my bulimia. Spirituality, a higher being or a cosmic force, whatever your own interpretation, it makes very little odds to me because whatever it was, I have found a common ground with it once more. Somewhere inside, something more compelling than my thoughts and more moving than my emotions was reawakened. It was like finding an ancient fossil buried deep in the earth of my very being. Finally, I had made my peace with God.

I'm sure I must make this all sound terribly easy; of course it wasn't. These processes were slow and I even doubted the likelihood of their success for the longest time. Blind hope was all that fuelled me. But having established a reasonable degree of reconciliation with my past and having worked through my quarrels with God, the time came when I was ready to put myself back together in some of the only ways I knew how. The first of these ways was through art. Having always had a flair when it came to wielding a pencil in my hand, my interest in the vast and eclectic world of art had grown steadily and healthily before I ever encountered such a thing as bulimia nervosa.

When I was about 14 years old, I recall working on a preparatory sheet for art class. It was something we were required to do for almost every piece of work we wished to submit and involved gathering personal sketches and perusing whatever images you could find to broaden the scope with which you drew. But that wasn't always easy because the scope with which I saw art at the time was very limited. I remember how desperately I had tried to understand it all, but just couldn't seem to get the grip of it; cubism, surrealism, impressionism or whatever other important sounding name they'd given it, I simply couldn't comprehend the art behind a painting or drawing that resembled a mashed up picture, which could have been done by a child. For the sake of 'knowing' art, I had tried very hard indeed but the pieces of this puzzle just didn't seem to fit with me for a very long time. Yet, amidst my internet searches and textbook page-flipping, I once came across a rather curious image. I kept returning to it again and again before finally looking at it properly, as if for the first time. Strangely disproportionate and unappealing to the eye, such an artwork was usually the very definition of the paintings I disliked the most. And yet, looking at that image in that moment, something caught me and consumed me entirely. The painting was entitled *St Francis Receiving the Stigmata* by an artist of the name El Greco.

The most striking thing in this painting was a most exuberant and shocking use of blue. There was something extraordinarily atmospheric about that blue, as if it was painted only from the artist's imagination, or as if the colour had never even existed before this image was created. This man, El Greco, seemed to own that colour in such a way that its purpose was dependent wholly upon what the artist's imagination dictated. As such, the blue could have easily been the sky, the mind, or even heaven, whatever the artist so wished of it. The painting was a vision of an internal and deeply spiritual event. Within this representation, it had a dreamlike quality that touched a part of me, which only came to life in my sleep. The imaginative portrayal depicted how St Francis *felt* in the given moment, rather than what was proportionally correct. The application of this emphasis added a new dynamic to what art – for me at least – was all about.

I looked at the figure of St Francis. His face was too gaunt, his belt tied too tightly to hold a body and his fingers bent themselves in such a manner that would surely have broken them in reality. Above him and shining down so gloriously was the light of the Holy Spirit, from whom the gaunt man – I momentarily – obsessed over was receiving the gift of the stigmata.

'Freedom from death', I remember reading beside the picture.

The stigmata was a reminder of freedom from death. And yet in contrast to this, I gazed downwards at the ghostly saint where sat a skull as a reminder of mortality which plagues us all. While entranced by this visual, something about it shook me in a cold chill. Until that point, I had never known paintings could do that, not really. A painting – or any artwork for that matter – was something that imitated life alone and anything outside of those realms was most certainly just an excuse for what it should have been. In my own naive understandings of art before that point, paintings were about craftsmanship and not expression. This, I had been certain of.

But El Greco was very much a man who lived inside his own head, with figures that simply could not have existed anywhere else. He was known to sit in darkness, neither asleep nor painting, simply imagining. His painting retained the capacity to evoke strong feelings and allow the viewer to experience an extraordinary moment in another person's life or perhaps even another world, as I believe I did that day. He was, in his own right, a revolutionary and changed my own personal ideology of what paintings should be.

As it turned out, El Greco would never go on to be an artist with whom I ever developed a particular interest or accord with. But I have never forgotten the day I stumbled across such a painting. It caused me to reconceptualise the purpose of art and the ways in which it may be best executed. In terms of my bulimia, art became a key factor in my attempts to rid myself of that voice that persisted in my head. I needed a distraction from her and the filthy thoughts with which she still haunted me. Rediscovering a then lost passion for art became one of the major stepping stones as I attempted to rebuild the person I had left behind so long before her. By the end of my time spent in therapy, I couldn't remember looking at a painting like that in about two or more years.

Passion, in this way, can feed the soul if allowed to erupt without constraint or restriction. It is more than just a notion or a belief. Passion is the rawest nerve within each of us that calls for expression in some form or another. I think I had forgotten what it was to be passionate about anything. Lethargy had long since riddled my understanding of the very word and stripped me of all its bearings. When the time was right, I finally sought to reignite that fervour, which lay dormant within the forgotten crevices of who I was beneath the bulimia.

A few months after therapy, I found myself sifting endlessly from image to image, in books that I had forgotten I had. But there they all were, as they had always been – Vermeer, Metsu, Renoir, Monet, Manet, Yeats – the list went on and on. They still had the glory that I first viewed each with. Every painting, shadow, curved line, hue of colour, texture of surface, impression and tone was met with an internal and emotional enthusiasm that only art itself could provoke. I couldn't remember fully why I started refreshing the visual memories of these artworks in my head but it didn't matter anyway because purpose always had very little to do with it.

While this process of 'rediscovering' myself through the realms of art was by and large a slow one, I do recall that one defining moment when I felt I had truly found myself once more. I have one artist in mind, whose visuals reflect raw emotion; both that of the artist himself and of whomever the given viewer fortunate enough to gaze at such work. I remember trying to say his name, as if saying it in just the right way would connect me to the person, as the painting had connected me to his art.

'Go,' I pronounced. 'Van Gooo.' No, it wasn't right.

'Goff', I started again. 'Van Goff, Van Gow.' Still not right.

'Vincent.'

Yes, that was correct. The world-renowned Vincent Van Gogh was, to me, just Vincent. And with that, I knew him and what's more, I knew myself in his reflection and in his art. Before his paintings, I temporarily stopped being everything I had known of myself. I stopped being a victim of bullying, I stopped being a fat little girl, I stopped being the production of rejection, I stopped being a student, writer and author, I even stopped being a bulimic. All cauterization and need for self-definition faded away. Yes, standing before his paintings, I was finally just Leanne.

During this period, as I continued to piece back together all the fragments of who I was – and without the crutch of Michelle and our weekly meetings – I also had to undergo a personal phase of evolution. What it entailed was accepting responsibility for my own illness. This isn't to say, accepting that it had all been my fault. Rather, it encompassed the idea of *owning* my disease. Only this way could I live with its many consequences. Part of owning my bulimia was facing, without hesitation or fear, the third parties it had hurt the most. These were my family and friends.

In terms of my friends, I felt like I owed them something of titanic measure. It was as if they had signed a contract of friendship, so many years ago, to a person who ultimately didn't uphold their end of the deal. The person they knew by the time my bulimia had fully consumed me was not the person they had signed up for so long ago. And while I acknowledge that people change, I had compromised my given path with these people by growing away from them instead of with them. I had broken our agreement and thus, owed them more than I thought I could give. One of my closest friends put it quite simply to me one day, she said, 'We don't *want* anything from you, Leanne. We just want you. We want you to just come back.' This was all I had to repay in all my debts. How very mind-boggling it was to me at the time. It was like I had taken out loan after loan on my personality and now that the time came to repay it all, my friends had simply defaulted the situation and allowed me to start from scratch again, with all the credit I had possessed before.

I sought to remember who I was in the context of these women and why we had been friends in the first place. I traced back through all the memories we had shared; every laugh, every summer day, every tear and every word we had uttered to one another. These women were more than friends; they were my soul mates, my comrades and all the goodness left in my heart. I took what was left of that heart and very gradually, they nurtured it once more. I paid my debt to them simply by letting them back in. It's still a miracle to me.

The hurt I had caused my family was irrevocable and worst of all, it was something I did not always witness or even know of. There could be no default with my family because relationships with our kin are just never that simple. For the most part, reconstructing my life within the family unit required a major shift in each of the relationships. All of them were in desperate need of open communication and a new awareness of the individuals that made up this one entity. This transition was never better seen than between my mother and I. In the beginning, the awkwardness that persisted was almost intolerable. We knew far too much about each other now. I had let her deep into my hidden shadows and she had shared things I was never sure I even wanted to hear. The entire episode once made me think of the parent-child sex talk. *That* is the level of awkwardness we are discussing here, only spread out over an excruciatingly long period of time. What it has resulted in since that time, simply, is a relationships based around honesty. With this in hand, most other things seem to fall into place, or at least this is what we always hope for anyway. It's a never-ending process because relationships themselves are ever changing. But the things we have both learned from this horror known as bulimia have – if nothing else – armed us for whatever is to come in future.

More than this, in some cases, I found I had to *start* relationships within my family too. My brother, who was seven years my senior, had featured very little in this part of my life and in my puberty-stricken years before then. Largely, this was just a result of age and circumstance; we would just never be on the same page because we each lived a different life until the other. And it would take years for that gap to even start balancing out. I still have only one image in my memory of my brother as a child and even at that, it's a most blurry one.

I AM VERY YOUNG, too young to even know I have an age at all or what that means. I'm crying in my room but don't entirely know why. I share a bedroom with Natalie. Squashed into our tiny abode are a set of bunk beds. I sleep on the top bed, while my sister sleeps on the one below. But our room is different now because there is a mattress on the floor. Mum has made it up with pillows and bed sheets. This is because my brother Peter must sleep in our bedroom, while his is being used for a student living with us for a month.

I don't remember Peter walking into the room, but in the middle of my crying, suddenly his face is an inch away from mine. He is pulling silly faces. He crosses his eyes back and forth, raises his brow up and down and stretches his mouth as wide as it can go, bearing all his teeth. He drops down on all fours and pretends to be *Scooby Doo*. At this, I start to laugh through my dying tears.

When I wipe the last of them away, Peter switches from dog to horse. He starts to neigh like a horse as loud as he can and I laugh uncontrollably. He plonks me atop his back and starts to trot around the tiny floor space, still neighing like a horse and shaking his head every time. I laugh until I fall off his back and onto the mattress on the floor, clutching my sides through the hysteria.

I can't remember Peter ever doing something like this before. Then again, I can't remember much of Peter at all before now. But as always, his presence is so familiar. I know him well somehow.

Though my brother was never completely out of my life, it was only around the time of my illness that we even began a coherent relationship with one another. Before that point, our relationship had been one of blood and very little else; or maybe I just can't remember. I often wondered whether my big brother would have preferred the old me or the me he was getting then. It didn't matter anyway because I couldn't change it, but it always lingered in the back of my head. It's a strange place to be when you begin getting to know a person you thought you knew your entire life.

The issue of my studies was another hurdle that I had to face throughout my 'regeneration.' I had never known that world without my bulimia and began my second year as a person not with an eating disorder, but as a 'bulimic in recovery.' It was only slightly more appealing than the former title at the time. I had a lot of making up to do in this area and threw myself into regaining some of my former academic glory. It was as if I had to teach myself all over again how one goes about learning and studying. It's still something I'm working on. But the hopes I once held so high in terms of my education remain what they had always been. I hadn't lost those ambitions as it would turn out, merely forgotten them for a while. Knowledge is empowering and with my education, I know that eventually, I may even hold the key to destroying her forever.

The issue of my self-worth was a topic dealt with extensively throughout my therapy. But the constant maintenance of a healthy perception of person and what qualifies me as a worthy person in this world is an ongoing endeavour. Every day, we are each presented with obstacles that can hinder, wound or severely damage us. My job for the time being is merely to overcome those obstacles in a healthy way and with a positive outcome. It sounds terribly simple when put into just one sentence like that. If only the reality were so easily dealt with. Then again, I've always been better with words than I have been with the life that inspires them.

Furthermore, the insecurities that so often surrounded the matter of men and my relationships came back to that concept of worth, time and time again. Only through the expansion and sincere inflation of my own worth have I been able to even mildly get a grasp on the relationships that they result in. But the truth is that, even in a stage of recovery or post recovery, my bulimia continues to affect my relationships with men. The most primitive way in which this can be seen is within just the admission of the eating disorder itself. She is still so meticulously intertwined into who I am that I cannot fully show myself to anyone without showing her too. There comes a point in any romantic relationship – if indeed, I wish for that romance to go any further – that she must step out of the shadows and into the light. Only when she is there can I be seen for all I am, both good and bad. Of course, this isn't exactly pillow talk and thus, still carries weight in any romantic undertaking. They cannot escape it, no more than I can.

The hardest part of reconstructing my life, which has been forfeited to an eating disorder, is letting go. Letting *her* go has been like letting go of an imperative part of myself. And every now and then, late in the morning hours of sleepless nights, I often feel the itch of temptation at the back of my neck. She may drift into my head, willing me to regress. Ignoring her can be painful; it can be upsetting; and equally, it can be liberating. How I will respond to her coaxing is just a matter of how the cards are dealt on any given day. But in general, I cannot bring myself to think of her as I once did. She had been the magnum opus of everything that was wrong with my life. She had never been my friend. And every time I think too about these things, I always come to one devastating realisation: there had never been a 'she.' She never existed because she had always been me.

I was my own darkness and it was about time I owned up to that truth and God forbid, even embrace it along with everything else; not because it causes any good, but just because it's a part of me as much as everything else.

Above my bed hangs a framed picture of Vincent Van Gogh's *Starry Night*. It is perhaps my favourite of all his paintings, though this is subject to change with my mood, just as his painting was subject to his own moods. He was an artist of complete emotion. His work was an expression of what he felt and who he was. They were paintings without fear. There remains a most definite darkness to the concept of mankind and what it stands for in terms of the globe and all the individuals who compose it. I remember thinking this while looking at that *Starry Night* not long before I began writing this memoir. I recall being struck, among a very long list of other things, by the bright colours of that painting. How the swirling movement of them gave life to the hands that created it and now the eyes that beheld it. But my eyes could not help but fall into the dark absence of colour from time to time in that painting. There was a profound darkness in it. And then I realised that the brilliance of those extravagant colours was encapsulated only in that darkness.

Without it, such colours could surely never be so bright or so beautiful. Equally, the shadows of mankind play a similar role in all of us. The perfection of uninterrupted colour in the paintings of our lives would most certainly make for a blinding picture. Without that darkness, we cannot fully see the glory of our own light. Without that darkness, perhaps we would see no light at all.

Let the darkness out and let the light in.

MORE NON-FICTION FROM MAVERICK HOUSE

EATING SMOKE

One Man's descent into drug psychosis in Hong Kong's triad heartland

BY CHRIS THRALL

Chris Thrall left the Royal Marines to find fortune in Hong Kong, but following a bizarre series of jobs ended up homeless and addicted to crystal meth.

He began working for the 14-K, one of Hong Kong's notorious crime syndicates, as a nightclub doorman in the Wan Chai red-light district.

Dealing with psychosis, conspiracy and the 'foreign triad' — a secretive expat clique that works hand-in-hand with the Chinese mafia — he had to survive in the world's most unforgiving city, addicted to the world's most dangerous drug . . .

"What else would you expect from a former Royal Marine Commando? Chris Thrall has a hell of a story to tell, and he does so with humour, candour and page-turning prose."

Tom Carter. *CHINA: Portrait of a People*

". . . exemplary pacing, completely engaging tone, wealth of winning detail. Thrall uses such verve, enthusiasm and faultless comic timing that it is hard not to be swept along."

South China Morning Post

To order this book go to www.maverickhouse.com

MORE NON-FICTION FROM MAVERICK HOUSE

A Deal with the Devil

The Green Party in Government

By Mary Minihan

The Green Party struck its "deal with the devil" by entering coalition with Fianna Fáil in 2007.

The junior partner secured control of the Environment and Energy ministries, irritating some in the larger party with its pursuit of a ban on stag hunting, the introduction of civil partnerships for same-sex couples and restrictions on planning.

An unprecedented crisis in the State's finances, with an exposure of the deeply flawed Irish banking system, shook the party's grassroots and its vote collapsed in the local and European elections in June 2009. The following October, party members threatened to pull out of Government over the controversial National Asset Management Agency (Nama), while senior figures were kept in the dark about the arrival of the IMF in 2010. The Greens dropped a bombshell late that year, demanding a date for an early general election, but stayed in Government in the hope of passing key Green legislation.

Controversy over revelations about then Taoiseach Brian Cowen's contacts with Sean Fitzpatrick while he was still Anglo chairman strained relationships further. A bungled reshuffle was aborted at the behest of the Greens, and the "momentous" decision to pull the plug on the Coalition was taken in January 2011. But their three-and-a-half year period in Government cost them dearly at the polls.

To order this book go to www.maverickhouse.com

MORE NON-FICTION FROM MAVERICK HOUSE

THE ANGEL OF BANG KWANG PRISON

By SUSAN ALDOUS

WITH NICOLA PIERCE

The inmates of Bang Kwang Prison in Bangkok rarely have anything to look forward to; except a visit from their own personal angel.

Susan Aldous had been on a path of self-destruction when she decided to give her life to others instead of wasting it away in Melbourne's dark underbelly.

Realising she wanted to help the poorest of the poor, Susan moved to Singapore and then to Thailand to work on a nine-day project helping the socially disadvantaged. She is still there 18 years later.

A single mother with no salary and few possessions, she devotes her life to helping others, bringing hope and humanity to the prison; one of the toughest places on Earth, among other projects.

Whether it is teaching young Thai men to accept the world they live in, or helping foreign inmates adjust to life in a Thai jail, Susan Aldous is a one-woman charity phenomenon. There are 7,000 inmates in the prison; all of them have heard of Susan, the 'Angel of Bang Kwang'.

This is her story.

To order this book go to www.maverickhouse.com

MORE NON-FICTION FROM MAVERICK HOUSE

Miss Bangkok

Memoirs of a Thai Prostitute

By Bua Boonmee

WITH Nicola Pierce

Miss Bangkok is a vivid, powerful and moving memoir of a life spent in prostitution in Thailand. Poor and uneducated, Bua Boonmee escaped an abusive marriage only to end up in the go-go bars of Patpong. There, in the notorious red-light district of Bangkok, she succumbed to prostitution in an effort to support her family.

Bua's story is one of resilience and courage in the face of abuse and poverty. Her confessions will make you laugh and cry, cringe and applaud. She will change your perception of prostitution forever.

To order this book go to www.maverickhouse.com